MERSEYSIDE'S
WAR

Voices of the First World War

MERSEYSIDE'S
WAR

Mike Benbough-Jackson

AMBERLEY

Surrendered German submarine, 1919. (Author's collection)

First published 2015

Amberley Publishing
The Hill, Stroud
Gloucestershire, GL5 4EP

www.amberley-books.com

Copyright © Mike Benbough-Jackson, 2015

The right of Mike Benbough-Jackson to be
identified as the Author of this work has been asserted in accordance
with the Copyrights, Designs and Patents Act 1988.

British Library Cataloguing in Publication Data.
A catalogue record for this book is available from the British Library.

ISBN 978 1 4456 3922 2 (paperback)
ISBN 978 1 4456 3933 8 (ebook)

Typesetting and Origination by Amberley Publishing
Printed in Great Britain

Contents

Acknowledgements

I'd like to thank the following for answering questions, indicating sources, and for their enthusiasm and inspiration while I was putting this book together: Professor John Belchem, Professor Gary Sheffield, Dr Helen Rogers, Dr Paul O'Leary, Jonathan Ali, Dr Neil Evans, David Hearn, Bill Sergeant, Jim Clarke, Sue Leuty, Brenda Murray, Karen O'Rourke, Will Meredith and Professor Maggie Andrews who drew my attention to the *Voices of the World War One* series. My colleagues on the 'Merseyside at War, 1914-1918' team at LJMU (Professor Frank McDonough, Dr Emma Vickers and Vicki Caren) have been on hand to help with queries and suggest sources. Take a look and contribute to the project website www.merseyside-at-war. org. The people who provided their stories and images for the website all conveyed an infectious enthusiasm for keeping alive an awareness of the war and its consequences. Among them I would like to thank Tom Carlin for permission to reproduce the image on p.209.

Librarians and archivists at the following institutions helped me dip into the past: Liverpool Central Library and Record Office, Crosby Library, Wirral Archives, Merseyside Maritime Museum, Birkenhead Library, St Helens Library, Leeds University Library, British Library, London, and the Imperial War Museum Archive. I would also like to thank the following repositories for granting permission to reproduce images from their collections: images 1, 2, 8, 15, 16, 17, 26 and 29 (Liverpool Central Library); images 3, 10, 24 and 28 (Wirral Archives); images 11 and 13 (Leeds University

Library); image 28 (St Helens Library). Every effort has been made to fulfil requirements with regard to reproducing copyright material. The publisher will be glad to rectify any omissions at the earliest opportunity.

Thanks also to my parents and Shân for reminding me of life beyond the screen-face.

Introduction

This book brings together numerous accounts drawn from diaries, parliamentary debates, letters, newspapers, local histories, local government records, oral histories, biographies and autobiographies. Some are from people who left Merseyside to serve in the conflict, while others are voices from the home front. There are also some accounts from people who passed through Merseyside during the war.

To understand the significance of the accounts that follow, it is important to acquire a sense of what defined Merseyside at the start of the twentieth century. At the same time, there is value in gaining some idea of how Merseyside's experience of the war has been seen by later writers.

As the 'second city of empire', Liverpool and its environs played a pivotal role in the war. The port was a place where supplies and raw materials entered the country and where manufactured products were exported. Ships were like red blood cells, carrying the oxygen of commerce to all parts of the globe. In all, by 1914 some 31 per cent of the goods that come in to the country and the products that were shipped overseas passed through the port.[1] Seeing as southern and eastern English ports were unable to function as normal during the war, Liverpool's docks were especially busy. Trade after the war would never reach the levels of the Edwardian era, but the war gave Liverpool a temporary, if artificial, boost. Later known as the 'three graces', the buildings of the Mersey Docks and Harbour Board (1907), Royal Liver (1908) and Cunard Office (1913) stood watch over a trade route that helped sustain Britain and its wartime allies.

The population of Merseyside in 1911 was almost 1,485,000.[2] Liverpool, with a population of 746,421, was the third most populous city in England, after London and Birmingham.[3] Most of the population depended on the trade that passed through Liverpool's docks for their livelihoods. Today, when the arrival and distribution of goods is barely acknowledged, it is difficult to grasp the significance of ships. For the people of Merseyside, they were a source of employment, income and pride.[4] Birkenhead, Ellesmere Port and Liverpool helped Britannia rule the waves. When Germany's submarines challenged Britannia's claim over the oceans, Merseyside was often the first to feel the loss of ships and their cargo. To take the example of just one company, Moss Steamship Co. of Liverpool lost fourteen ships to U-boat action during the conflict.[5]

Perhaps there is no better indication of the importance of Merseyside to the health and wealth of Britain than the reports in the German press. When she described the effect of the Zeppelin raids, Mrs Humphry Ward wrote that the Germans were being 'fed on ridiculous lies about the destruction of Liverpool docks and the wreaking of "English industry"'.[6] The *Hamburger Nachrichten* may have been wrong – as was the Zeppelin captain who thought part of the Midlands was Merseyside – but the erroneous report that described the 'bombardment' of Liverpool docks is a revealing fiction. Merseyside mattered.

This artery of the British Empire contained a huge variety of people engaged in numerous occupations. There were the working classes, who were employed in a variety of jobs, some of which were skilled professions, such as the shipbuilding in Birkenhead, and others, which were less skilled and unsecure forms of employment, like the manual labour on the docks. Others were occupied in traditional industries like agriculture or the service industries – such as the leisure trade in Southport and

New Brighton. Tensions between employer and employee during the Edwardian era resulted in Liverpool's transport strike of 1911, where some 80,000 gathered in protest and two men were killed by the army.[7] Conflicts of interest between workers and their employers continued during the war.

The middle classes tended to live on the outskirts of the city or across the river on Wirral and were as varied as the working classes. Some worked in offices, ran businesses or were professionals. Among their number were men and some women who stimulated the region's sporting culture. If they were not already members of the territorial force, amateur cricket and rugby players were often among the first to join the military during the war. A number of middle-class women were active in the campaign for the right to vote. Dr Alice Kerr, a Birkenhead physician, was among the women who attacked properties in Kensington High Street, London on 4 March 1912.[8] These suffrage campaigns contributed to the often tense atmosphere of Edwardian Liverpool.

There were a variety of ethnic groups that gave Merseyside, and Liverpool in particular, a distinctive character. Chinese, South Asian and West African sailors passed through the city and some stayed in or around what was known as 'sailortown'.[9] In addition, there were large numbers of people who were passing through the port on the way to or from other countries. According to the 1911 census, on census night 1.4 per cent of the population of Liverpool were foreign-born subjects. This proportion would have been considerably higher in areas towards the centre of the city. Its proximity to Ireland, Wales and Scotland meant that Merseyside contained a significant number of people from the Celtic fringe. The Mersey was the route to and from the Atlantic, and accents and languages from around the world could be heard on its shores.

This diversity was represented by the the different religious buildings dotted around the region. The Catholic churches served a large number of Irish migrants, while a range of Protestant institutions catered for denominations that ranged from the Unitarians to the Anglican Church. For the most part, relations were amicable between the Catholic and Protestant portions of the population. Yet clashes between Orangemen and Catholics in Liverpool during 1909 led to a Home Office inquiry. The following year, there were clashes in St Helens. National divisions over Home Rule for Ireland were reflected in Liverpool. T. P. O'Connor, an Irish Nationalist, held the Liverpool Scotland constituency in a city that had a strong Tory tradition embodied by the staunch Unionist Archibald Salvidge. Towards the end of March 1914, a local newspaper was informed that some 3,000 armed Irish Nationalists from Liverpool were prepared to travel to Ulster to fight for Home Rule.[10]

Such tensions, along with class conflict, meant that Merseyside was a microcosm of the troubles that shook Edwardian England. At the same time, however, the port of Liverpool and its hinterland reflected the confidence of the world's largest empire. These shaped Merseyside's war. Each part of Britain, just like every individual, experienced the war in a different way.

Those who write about the past, not only professional or amateur historians but novelists, poets, journalists, politicians and others, have written a great deal about the First World War. Perhaps it is better to say that they write about *their* First World War. For even those who lived through the conflict are influenced by the sources that have been consulted, as well as current personal and social concerns. As a result, some topics are given more attention than others, as are some debates and differences of opinion. Most of the current observations about Merseyside and the war either focus on selected military aspects or the social history of the home front.

A number of official regimental histories of the war were written fairly soon after the conflict ended. With the burgeoning interest in genealogy, however, there has been more focus on the lives of individuals who served in the army. Attention often falls on those who died or were awarded medals. Men who volunteered and the units they formed, such as the Liverpool Pals and the Cheshire Bantams, have also been given consideration. There were many others, notably the conscripts, whose stories either do not possess the same allure, or who have not left sufficient records. Business historians have noted the effects of the war on shipping companies and the docks, but given Merseyside's association with the sea it is surprising that more has not been published about the sailors and merchant seamen from the area.

While noting what happened to soldiers, sailors and airmen during the war helps us answer the question 'what happened?', it is only the first step towards answering the kinds of questions raised by those academic historians who are interested in the effect of the war on the identities of those who fought and the extent to which soldiers and sailors felt isolated from the communities they left behind. Such questions help us get closer to finding out how people lived and thought during the war. Fortunately, there are two studies that use Liverpool to explore these issues. Helen McCartney examined the experiences of Territorial soldiers from the port and surrounding area who fought in the war, while Michael Finn looked at local newspapers and noted how local war heroes were reported to communities. Both McCartney and Finn argue that there was a closer connection between the home front and battle front than many have assumed.[11] This book provides examples from a variety of sources that address and contextualise the important questions of how the war affected those who lived through the conflict.

Studies dedicated to the region's home front have been few and far between, and have generally taken a descriptive approach to social history rather than one that tries to make sense of the war on the home front.[12] Opinions about the conflict are scattered throughout a variety of studies that deal with labour history, women's history and general histories of Liverpool and Merseyside. *Merseyside's War* will draw many of these perspectives together and relate them to one another.

Merseyside's experience of the war has not been ignored. But this book provides glimpses of situations and opinions that both broaden and deepen our appreciation of the region during the First World War. Indeed, the examples within its pages help us get up close to the people and events of the period and learn about what made people happy, angry, smile and cry.

1

Men and the War

Less than a month into the war, Kitchener's call for volunteers had been answered by hundreds of thousands of men. Many in Liverpool were proud of the city's contribution to the 'New Army'. The example set by leading figures in the city was highlighted. In the streets, bands played music to stir the spirit and display the smart, orderly appearance of a soldier on parade. As well as proclaiming the ideals of patriotism, the authorities paid attention to practical issues. Men needed to be transported and equipped. This report from the end of August comes at the start of what has been described as the 'first rush' to the colours between 25 August and 15 September 1914.[1] Liverpool was already playing its part in the call to arms before the formation of the Pals, which the Earl of Derby suggested to the War Office on 24 August.

When the new Liverpool battalion takes its completed shape it will be found that amongst its officers are represented many well-known local families, who thus show themselves as ready for patriotic service as in peaceful times they are ready for the work of social advancement.

Over the week-end the recruiting was particularly brisk, and in less than a week as many as 1,000 men have been enrolled, which is a number larger than that actually required for the constitution of the 11th 'King's'. The War Office have now sent orders for the recruiting to be continued, and efforts are to be redoubled so as to form one more battalion, and it is hoped that an equally speedy announcement of this being done can be sent to Lord Kitchener.

Lord Kitchener's offer to act as the colonel-in-chief of the new battalion is [a] notable one. Liverpool, indeed, is practically the first place to enrol a complete unit in connection with his lordship's special army, and that is the more remarkable when it is remembered how many local men are already serving their country. Lord Kitchener has acknowledged this splendid rally by becoming colonel-in-chief, and that this is no idle reward from a man who has no time for mere distinction-bestowing is clear from the fact that the only other regiment in the British Army which he has honoured in this way is the corps in which he served so many years – that of the Royal Engineers.

The Seaforth Barracks expect to continue active, and more motor-cars are asked for so that men who present themselves at one of the collecting depots, situated in all parts of the city and district, can be transferred to the barracks. Last night an incidental effort to further the recruiting was the playing of patriotic music outside the recruiting office in Old Haymarket, to which the band marched with waving flags and accompanied by cheering crowds from St. James's-place, and then marched back to the depot in Scotland-road. While no funds have been asked for, it is stated that cheques have been received from Lord Derby, Lord Sefton, Mr J. Rankin, and Mr A. Powlett. This money will be placed to the reserve fund of the Old Comrades' Association, which has done so much admirable work since it was founded only three years ago by Major Warrington.

It is stated officially that no bounty will be paid to ex-soldiers on joining Lord Kitchener's new army. In accordance with the usual custom, however, a bounty will, it is expected, be paid at the termination of hostilities.[2]

Fighting clerks: some of the first to sign up were from Liverpool's stock exchange. (Courtesy of Liverpool Record Office, Liverpool Libraries 332/LSE/7/4)

J. Finch   C. V. Jones   Charles G. Mann

After the 'first rush' of late August and early September, further efforts were made to attract volunteers. One of those who called on Liverpool to contribute more troops was Winston S. Churchill. In his speech at Tournament Hall on 21 September 1914, the First Lord of the Admiralty was optimistic. He stressed the potential of the empire and the role of the navy. Churchill's praise for the navy reflects the widely held belief that Britain's role in the war would be to maintain mastery of the sea while her allies fought on the continent.[3] As it turned out, Britain would contribute millions of troops to the conflict on land. Churchill's comments about a purely volunteer force and that the conflict would be over in a matter of months turned out to be wildly inaccurate. Yet others held similar views, including the German-born but anti-German British diplomat Eyre Crowe and the British ambassador in Berlin, Edward Goshen.

Mr Chairman and Gentlemen: It is well that the force and spirit of all the classes and interests in the British Empire are all flowing together into one great channel, and moves forward to the realization of the whole strength of the British people. The times in which we live are terrible; the course of events has passed outside the boundaries of the most daring imagination. The actual facts are so stunning, the scale of all the phenomena presented to our view are so vast, that we can only feel, each one of us, that we must just lay hold of the next obvious simple step which duty indicates. [Cheers.] How we shall reach the end we cannot see now. But the immediate step before us we can see quite plainly. [Cheers.]

I have not come here to ask you for your cheers: I have come to ask you for a million men for the gallant Army of Sir John French – a million of the flower of your manhood, nothing but the best, every man a volunteer – [Cheers] – a million men maintained in the field and equipped with everything that science can invent or money can buy ...

My friendship with Mr F. E. Smith [who was about to leave his post as Director of the Government Press Bureau] is one of the most cherished possessions of my life, and I am glad to be on this platform with him. In a few days he is off to the war – [great cheering] – and I join with you in wishing that he may come back when matters have been satisfactorily adjusted. [Cheers.] ...

So far as the Navy is concerned, we cannot fight while the enemy remains in port ... if they do not come out and fight they will be dug out like rats in a hole. [Cheers.] Under the shield of our Navy you can raise an army in this country which will settle the war within six or seven months ...

I became responsible for this great department of the Navy, and I have had to see every day evidence of the espionage system which Germany maintained in this country ... Every dirty little German lieutenant – [laughter] – coming on leave to England has thought he would curry favour with his superior by writing home details of where water can be got, where there is a blacksmith's forge, how much provisions there may be for a battalion or a brigade in this village or that township of our peaceful island. We have been subjects of a careful and deliberate scientific military reconnaissance ...

Peace will be found, in the words of his Majesty the King, when the worthy causes for which we are fighting have been fully achieved. We may live to see the Christian states of the Balkans restored to their proper racial limits; we may see Italy's territory correspond with her Italian population; we may see France restored to her proper station in Europe and in her rightful place; and we may see that Old England had something to do with it all. If these results be achieved, the million men will not have been demanded or supplied in vain. [Cheers.][4]

A month after Churchill's rousing oratory at Tournament Hall, the MP for West Derby William Rutherford spoke in the House of Commons about concerns among recruits from his constituency. Their enthusiasm had been dampened by an absence of weapons and pecuniary matters. What is more, these territorial troops thought that they had been treated less fairly than other soldiers, both before and after leaving for training in Blackpool. Rutherford's question demonstrates how patriotism did not mean that men were not counting their pennies or prepared to put aside their pride.

Indeed, the territorials may have felt more entitled to fair treatment because they were serving before the war. Perhaps these territorial soldiers were all the more prepared to complain because they were often from the lower-middle classes. Kitchener once referred to them as the 'town clerks' army'.[5]

Mr Rutherford asked the Financial Secretary to the War Office whether he is prepared to take any steps to meet the grievances of some Liverpool men, a typical case of which is that of a man who enlisted at 65, St. Anne's Street, Liverpool, on the 2nd September, signed on for foreign service, has been sent to and is now at Blackpool, and has not yet fired a rifle; whether anything can be done to give this man and others similarly situated the necessary rifle training and the option of joining a battalion for active service; whether he is aware that the railway companies are charging full fare to many of these men between Blackpool and Liverpool when they get leave; whether, as there are a number of married men in the same position who only receive Is 9d a week (5s 3d being allotment money), he will consider the possibility of arranging that they shall not be charged 6s 9d railway fare; will he say whether steps were taken to avoid many of these men being compelled to wear their own clothes and boots, in some cases for nine weeks, seeing that other corps in Liverpool received allowances for the same; why these men did not receive kit allowance, which is supposed to be at the rate of 2d per day; whether he is aware that most of these men were kept ten weeks in Liverpool before being sent to Blackpool, during which period they had to sleep at home, there being no accommodation at the shed except for twenty men, and during that period they have had to pay for their own breakfasts every day and all meals on Sunday; whether the War Office has paid to the unmarried men only allowance for bed, breakfast, and Sunday meals; and, if so, will he explain why the married men are compelled to pay for these things themselves?

Mr. Baker: If the hon. Member will give me particulars of the names and units referred to I will have inquiries made. I may, however, state generally, that rifles are issued to Territorial Force soldiers as soon as they are available. Arrangements have been made to enable soldiers proceeding on leave to get tickets at half-fares. Men who wear their own civilian clothing are entitled to 3*d* a day up to a maximum of 7*s* 6*d*, which is about to be increased to 15*s* kit allowance at the rate of 2*d* a day is issuable from the 1st of September or date of enlistment, if later. Both married and unmarried men who are required to sleep at their own homes receive lodging allowance, and when they have to find some meals for themselves they receive either food in kind or an appropriate money allowance, or both.[6]

It is difficult to know what men did during their last days as civilians. Even diaries and memoirs do not tell us everything. Most would have made sure they said their goodbyes to loved ones and colleagues. Some would have prayed, possibly at a place of worship. There would have been opportunities for the more outgoing to announce their imminent departure in public houses, and as a result receive a few drinks. Rumours would have circulated about life in the army, as would the recollections of war veterans from the Crimean War to the Second Boer War. These men were at the watershed between civilian and military life. While some would have been reassured by what they heard, others would have had doubts about their decision to join up. But court reports show how some men got up to all kinds of antics before they left for the army. The first of the following extracts refers to a theft and is relatively innocent. However, the latter is more sinister. Leaving home could encourage men to commit acts of spite or vengeance. In both cases, the authorities appeared to be relatively unconcerned.

The war is not without its humorous side. A man was apprehended in Liverpool yesterday for being in a state of intoxication. He had in his possession a 55lb weight. Asked to account for it, he said 'I am going to enlist to-morrow to go to the war and I am taking this as a keepsake.'

Brought before the stipendiary to-day, Mr. Stuart Deacon asked, 'Will you enlist to-day if I discharge you?'

'Yes, sir,' the man replied readily, and he was thereupon discharged.[7]

At Garston Police court on Tuesday, before Messrs' A. E. Jacob and W. B. Stoddart, Nellie Walls, 16, Shand Street, Garston, was summoned for disorderly behaviour in St. Mary's road on Sunday night, the 20th December, Summonses had also been issued against two youths, but they had not been served, wrong names and addresses having been given.

Plain clothes officer Roberts said that about nine o'clock the defendant Walls, together with several youths and girls was behaving in a disorderly way. The youths were pulling the girls' hair and jostling, and people had to leave the footwalk to pass. The conduct was going on for about ten minutes.

Defendant said she was going down the village with a girl friend when two young men stopped them. They had drink in them and they wanted to get away. One wanted to keep her company but she did not want him. The officer said he had tried his best to find the young fellows and had been out to Oglet and Halewood where they said they lived, but could not trace them. Several youths from Oglet had joined the Army last week and they might have been among them.

The Chairman advised Walls and her friend who was in court to be more careful in future and keep clear of such men. The summons would be dismissed this time.[8]

Not everyone volunteered for the same reason. It is too simplistic to describe those who joined as naïve youngsters infected by war fever. Emotion and what would today be called peer pressure played a part, but so did a sense of duty. Joining the military enabled the volunteer to become a symbol of the values that were seen to embody British society.[9] Economic motives also played a part in the decisions taken by those who were in poorly paid or irregular work. Male family members set an example to their relatives, as did work males or fellow students. The battlefront and family life also influenced recruitment. Reports about the Battle of Mons on 23 August are thought to have stimulated the first great rush to the army. Not only was that battle seen as a victorious retreat, it brought home the reality of the war to many on the home front.

Published five days before Mons, this report called men to join in order to keep up with the efforts other cities. Economic, sporting and cultural competition between cities was a familiar feature of Victorian and Edwardian times, but now commitment to the war effort presented another means to outdo provincial rivals.

Throughout the length and breadth of the United Kingdom recruiting for the army services is progressing briskly. The response to Lord Kitchener's call to arms has so far been quite up to expectations in most of the large industrial centres of the country. Towns both great and small are vieing with each other in a patriotic endeavour to come out at the top of the recruiting tree.

Liverpolitans must look to their laurels, or else they will find themselves lagging behind other cities of lesser importance. Recruiting in the city shows no sign of a falling off, but it must not be forgotten that special efforts are being made in other parts of the country, so that it behoves every able-bodied man who can be spared to prove his patriotism by joining the colours.

There appears to be some misunderstanding in some quarters as to the terms of service. It should be explained that men are being enrolled for general service for a period of three years or the duration of the war. That is to say, if when the war is over they desire to leave the Army they are free to do so. On the other hand, they may elect to remain with the colours for the full three years, should the war not last so long.

Below we give an appeal to the patriotism of the citizens of Liverpool and district from Captain R. J. Finch, the local recruiting staff officer, who says:

'The Liverpool recruiting offices will be open on Sundays as on every other day. An extra recruiting office will be open on Sunday next at 56, Park-place, South-end. Captain Finch, R.S.O., Liverpool, appeals to the men of the city to come forward in greater numbers than hitherto, as otherwise some large towns and cities may beat Liverpool in the number of recruits presenting themselves for service during the war. Captain Finch feels that knowing the men of Liverpool from personal experience, both during peace and war, to be 'second to none,' they would, he is positive, feel this keenly were it to come to pass. The response to the call to arms to defend our beloved King and country has up to the present been splendid, but there is a risk of a falling off in numbers under the impression that enough men have been enrolled, therefore the recruiting staff officer considers it his duty to set the facts clearly, and he appeals to the men of Liverpool to remember the 'Roll of Honour' which is being compiled in his office, of the gallant fellows of Liverpool who have answered the call, and whose relatives and descendants may speak of with pride now, and in long years to come, as men who in the country's need did their duty to the land of their birth as true Britishers.

All honour to the brave. God save the King.

B. J. Finch, Captain, R.S.O.'[10]

Universities also vied with one another. Educational institutions were important recruiting grounds. Both schools and universities fostered national values and a sense of patriotism. This is not to say students were brainwashed. These institutions provided an environment where pre-existing ideals were magnified. There was a widely held belief that the well educated should play a part in leading society in peace and war. We tend to associate the students of the 1960s and 1970s as being opposed to war, so it is difficult for us to think of students as being among the loudest supporters of the war. However, both the anti-Vietnam War protestor and the eager recruit in the First World War were swept up by some of the dominant values of their day. Both felt they were doing their duty. This letter to Liverpool's Guild of Undergraduates magazine illustrates concern about the university's reputation and competition with another northern institution. The editors' comments after the letter are also revealing as it shows that this concern was not shared by all. Moreover, the comment about the 'fair sex' demonstrates an interest in gender matters that were also to the fore at the time.

Dear Sir,

It is with considerable surprise that I note the fact that only 130 out of (I believe) about 550 present students of the University are now serving with the colours, while Leeds, which is a smaller University, has furnished double the number. Why does Liverpool lag behind in this lamentable manner?

An attempt is made to remedy this shortage by a system of voluntary drill which at the best can be nothing else than miserably inadequate.

Might I suggest a far better method? A fourth Pals' Battalion is being formed. Let *every* able-bodied undergraduate enlist and form a strong Varsity contingent, such as we have in the 3rd Battalion. Let undergraduates do their obvious duty and set an example to all the other young men, and let the fair sex bring all possible pressure to bear upon those who are backward in answering their country's call.

Yours truly, Left marker.

[We think our correspondent's surprise is unnecessary. Does he know the private affairs of every member of the University? If so, why? Also is the proportion of the 'fair sex' in both Universities the same? By the way, which is the 'fair sex'? – Editors.][11]

The following brief messages home, published in a chapel magazine, contain snapshots of the war. The first two come from servicemen who had received parcels as a result of a button badge scheme. The badges became fashionable and were worn on ladies' hats and blouses. The young members of Crescent Congregational Chapel, Everton Brow, shared news and cartoons in a lively publication that has the appearance of what would later be called fanzines. The magazine contains reports from India, the Middle East, and both the western and home fronts. In general, the contents of the magazine were uplifting and would have reassured readers about their friends abroad. There are frequent references to home and other members of the congregation. The practice of underlining the names of people would have helped readers identify those who they knew and be reassured that they were well. While trench magazines enabled troops to forge communities while at war, magazines like *Young Crescent: Near and Far* sustained communities that had existed before the war.

Pte W. J. Aspinall (France) Sept. 6th 'The parcel's contents were of vital importance to me, because at the time of receiving, I had been inoculated + could not leave the billet. The cooker came in very handy indeed as the person sleeping on my left was unable to move. I was able to obtain some eggs for him from a farmhouse in the same yard as the billet, but as no fire was to be had the cooker and mess tin were immediately put into action, so the sick man was able to enjoy his first meal that day. The button is a lovely piece of work. Thanks for your thoughtfulness. Remembrance to all.'

Cyclist Bob Wilson (France) Sept. 20th. 'A better selection could not have been sent. Thanks! As regards roads I suspect you have seen photos of waggons stuck in the mud – well we are often in the same state. In fact, the bike has been thrown in the ditch + called for several days later. We are having a better time now than the first 12 months but that is not saying a great deal. I have had 26 months in this country, + don't like it any better now than the first month. Poor old Fritz must be having a bad time of it. I would not like to be on his side of the line. I am in the best of health. The only Crescent chap I have seen is Ted Singleton + that was just a glance and a yell as our trains passed. Hope things at Crescent are going strong.'[12]

Pte Alf Singleton (France) Oct 20th. 'My brother Fred has not been wounded, but gassed, + he has been lucky enough to get to Blighty, tho' a long way from home. I enjoy reading YC and you have a good artist in Mr. Williams. I pass the mag on to a friend of Miss Jessie Dunn who is in my brigade. It brings back memories of my younger days at Crescent, as I carry a souvenir of the gyms in the loss of my two front teeth! It has grieved me very much to read that some of the lads have made the great sacrifice, but I hope there will be no more. Good luck to the Crescent and all its classes.'[13]

Pte Ted Kneale (Rame France) July 4th 'During the last couple of months we have been roaming about 'sunny France' (it lived up to its name lately) by foot, bus and rail. I think I have seen more of France in the last 3 months, than in all the previous months over here. Luckily we've had very good weather, so the fact of having no roof on many recent occasions has not worried us at all. We've been in some very pretty parts too lately, but 'France is France for a' that.' I was very sorry to hear of the death of Geo. Strawson. England has been hit badly, but the spirit of the homefolk seems still as splendid as ever. I've often thought of Cornwallis St. when we've been footing it along the hot dusty roads. I could just do a cold plunge there now (what hopes?). It is hard enough at present to get a drop for a shave – in fact it is a tramp's paradise. Still smiling.'[14]

Men from opposite ends of the social spectrum served their king and country. All the workhouses on Merseyside appear to have supplied men for the war effort. As well as being clothed and fed, those who left the workhouse would have increased both their self-respect and respect from others. From this report, it appears that a number of these recruits were men who had already served in the forces. Private S. Baldrick in the comedy *Blackadder Goes Fourth* who hailed from the 'Turnip Street Workhouse Pals' may indeed have been 'a joke at the expense of the real British Pals battalions of 1914', but he also told a truth about those workhouse inmates who joined the colours.[15] Later those who were traumatised by the war could end up in the workhouse or the asylum.[16]

The call of King and country has even penetrated the walls of our poor-law institutions, and thousands of soldiers and naval reserves have been recruited from the inhabitants of the workhouses of the United Kingdom. From the four unions of Liverpool district – West Derby, the Parish of Liverpool, Toxteth, and Birkenhead – close upon 300 men have gone forth to join the colours.

No compulsion has been laid upon them. They have volunteered quite freely, and from the reports which are received they are making brave and efficient fighting men.

The West Derby Union – the largest poor law authority in the kingdom – has probably furnished a greater number of men than any

Humour and a hint of war-weariness in *Young Crescent*. (Courtesy of Liverpool Record Office, Liverpool Libraries M285CRE/7/6)

other single union. At Belmont Road on the outbreak of war the superintendent assembled the most vigorous-looking men of eligible age and gave them a friendly talk on the duties of patriotism. Thirty or forty ex-Army and Navy men soon expressed their willingness to serve, and without further ado they were packed off to the nearest recruiting station. From the other compatible men a company of about eighty were selected. A recruiting sergeant was called in, and he reduced the number to about fifty; and four-fifths of these men were sworn in at the Old Haymarket Station.

Since then, in ones and twos, recruits to the number of about thirty have responded to the duties of citizenship; indeed, so excellent is the spirit displayed by the men that it is claimed that there is not at the present moment a single man remaining in the institution who would be accepted by the Army or Navy if he presented himself. The same eagerness to serve their country in the hour of need has been exhibited in the other institutions.[17]

There is no doubt that for some a sense of duty, or desperation, was combined with a taste for adventure and a desire to experience combat. The following examples capture the allure of combat. This is not to say that these are honest, accurate portrayals of the battlefield. They are doubtlessly exaggerated statements of bravado. But the idea of combat and how it embodied values as varied as determination and physical prowess played a part in how the war was seen as well as experienced. The fact that many men avoided combat, through what has been called the live-and-let-live system, does not mean that there was not a prevailing idea of how men *should* act.[18] At the same time, both the experience and prospect of violence could cause the soldiers to bond, as they shared intense experiences that compelled them to rely upon one another. In the first example below, this shared experience among soldiers is reinforced by a common place of origin. As they exchanged tales of the fight afterwards, there would have been exaggeration and friendly rivalry. In many ways, these post-combat accounts helped men deal with the trauma; it is probably no coincidence that the

28

first account came from a wounded soldier. The letters in the second example have a positive tone that would have reassured a mother and father who had three sons in the army.

Graphic stories of the recent work of the Cheshire Regiment on the Western Front are told by a Birkenhead non-commissioned officer, now in a South of England hospital. In an interview, he said:

'The Cheshires have seen plenty of life since they got out there; and if they have seen life the Germans have seen death. I will never forget the night I got my ticket punched for "Blighty." The Huns were around us like swarms of locusts in Egypt. They were into us right and left, front, and nearly rear. Before they attacked they had pounded us for all they were worth with their big guns, and I thought for a time we were never going to get out of it.

'The gunfire ceased after a time, and the Kaiser's pets began their attack, three separate places at once. The first batch jumped our parapet and landed right on top of us. The fight that followed was of the old-fashioned primitive man style, with no fancy weapons to help us out. It was fists, fingers, nails, and feet all at it, and all in it at the same time; and it was warm work, I can tell you. Some of the Germans went further and bit at us as we grabbed them by the throat or caught them in the strangle-hold.

'There was nearly an hour of this hard scrapping before we cleared out what was left of the Huns. After that my company, mostly made up of Congleton chaps, with a few Birkenhead lads by way of seasoning, was moved forward to lend a hand at another part of the position where the enemy were playing red hell without any lid. It was there that the real fight was going on, for the enemy had poured up their finest troops, and had very nearly surrounded two companies of Cheshires. There were over 6,000 of the Huns and not 600 of us, so that the odds were terribly against us – at least 10 to 1. All the same, I enjoyed the scrap, and so did most of us.

'The Germans tried to force their way through our communication trenches with a lot of machine-guns. At one time there were only about fifteen of our boys to stop their game in that direction. These fifteen

– all from the Congleton district – lined up across the trench, and dared the Huns to come on. For nearly half an hour they held the Huns in check in spite of the fact that every man was wounded, and only retired when there was no further need for their services there. Four times in succession the Germans rushed one post, but each time we won it back, and finally held it.

'Towards night the position began to look critical at another point, where not two hundred of our lads were holding on against the third German attacking column, made up of crack Guardsmen, brought forward to arrest our advance at a point where it was threatening the retreating enemy.

'Our lads had got a proper gruelling, and were beginning to feel the strain. One of our officers, seeing what was happening, and seeing also another big German rush coming, called out 'Cheero, Cheshires! Give them hell!' And they got it. That cheerful word put new life into our men. They withstood the onslaught of the Kaiser's crack troops, and finally counter-attacking in turn, they hurled the foe back in disorder.'[19]

Formby is naturally proud of having contributed so large a quota to the Imperial Forces. Its roll of honour does credit to a small township, and at least one family has sent every member eligible to serve. Three sons of Mr and Mrs John Mawdsley, Coronation-avenue, are with the colours. Pte Harry Mawdsley has been in the 7th King's four years, and Pte Thomas Mawdsley two years. They left for the front about three weeks ago, and below we print part of the letters received from them. Pte John Mawdsley went into training with the 15th Battalion of the 1st King's at Freshfield a few weeks ago, and is disappointed at this training being interrupted with a twisted knee.

'April 2nd 1915,

'Dear Mother, I write these few lines hoping you are all keeping well, as the same leaves our Harry and me at present ... We had a splendid day here on April 1st. It was like a summer's day, the larks singing above. It was glorious, the finest day we have had ... We went in the trenches about seven o'clock. We expected the Germans making an attack, but it never came off, because perhaps they know what was waiting for them – good old 7th King's. The German's [*sic*] don't half shell round our little cottage, but they never hit it. I thought every minute it was going to be pitched down to the ground. After we have finished our job at night we get tea, and then we all sit round our little log fire telling a few tales and singing. When we went in the trenches the other day we could see a few Germans lying dead just outside our firing line. They were very big chaps, about six to seven feet in height. When the Germans started shelling yesterday they injured a few Frenchmen, and two or three out of the 5th King's down the main street. I think that is the most dangerous thing about the shelling ... Your ever loving son, Tom.'

'It is Good Friday to-day, and the weather is glorious, so I am lying in the field adjoining the house to write this letter. We have had another turn in the trenches, and all came back safe, but were lucky to avoid a casualty. At present the situation is fairly good, and we are all as well as can be expected ... There is one comfort here, and that is the strong opinion of a sudden end to it all ... The position which we are in is well watched by some hot stuff, but we can beat them every time, and we are itching for a bayonet charge ... Your loving son, Harry.'[20]

Our perception of the war is shaped by what we read. While some escapades read like fiction, Herbert Adams' diary entries convey the mundane nature of war along with some of the dangers of life in the trenches. In general, diaries tended to be bleaker than the letters soldiers sent home because there was no need to reassure the reader that all was well.[21] In November 1915, at the age of twenty, Adams joined the Liverpool 6th Rifles. A Baptist, he took a pocket bible his sweetheart Eveline Walker gave him in 1916 before he left for France. Inside the bible she wrote 'To Herbert from Evie "I will never forsake thee" May 8 1916'. Although Herbert was wounded twice, at Flers on the Somme in September 1916 and while crossing the Canal du Nord in September 1918, he survived the war. Nonetheless, his diary entries are poignant reminders of how he felt about his situation at the time. The poor weather, mud, lack of sleep, fleas and hunger were combined with inspections, drill and enemy shelling. Adams is often tired and finds the battle with mud and dust before inspection very difficult. His faith and letters from home sustained him through troubled times.

Sunday 11 June 1916

First Sunday in trenches – carry on as usual – rumour of being relieved.

Tuesday 13 June 1916

Chums go louse hunting.

Wednesday 14 June 1916

Biscuits and tinned fruit – plenty of bread & butter from home

Friday 16 June 1916

Squad Drill at chateau – afternoon off clean equipment etc & have a high tea. Some stunt [small operation] carrying water – almost done in. Loose [*sic*] way in trenches.

Saturday 17 June 1916

Bed down at 4am. Rose at 9am. Clean self up & do a bit of bayonet fighting. Squadron of Hun aeroplanes overhead. Lazy afternoon.

Sunday 18 June 1916

3.45am arrive at Beaumetche [Beaumetz] – ready for sleep. Slumbers disturbed by orderly corporal. 9am Church parade. Feel washed out have a sleep afternoon.

Monday 19 June 1916

Me on parade without cleaning rifle get sat on – new rifles issued busy clean up

Wednesday 21 June 1916

Wrote Mother have a bath – so far had no fleas on my shirt

Tuesday 22 June 1916

Still feel lazy & after 2 whole nights sleep. Do some physical and feel [fell?] out of training, humping a pack appears more natural – feel a bit out of sorts

Friday 23 June 1916

Fire ten rounds with new rifles & have a lazy morning – wrote Mother and Evie. Have a quiet evening – smoking etc.

Saturday 24 June 1916

Lose touch and flounder about on my own in mud & slush eventually reaching Mill St. Rain wet thro'.

Sunday 25 June 1916

Dirt from head to foot.

Monday 26 June 1916

Get back to billet 5am and bed down – too tired for breakfast.

Tuesday 27 June 1916

Iam shelled. Scuttled down to cellar post haste but stopped to put boots and steel helmet on.

Wednesday 28 June 1916

3.30am arrive in billet, expected breakfast failed to arrive. Sleep until Ipm and then scrape some of the dust off – start off to throw bombs during 2 hour bombardment.

Saturday I July 1916

2am roused. 3am start off. Pick up smoke bombs to Mill St. Game starts at 7.30. Fast and furious. Hughie Murdock and a sergeant killed. How wonderfully has God protected me. Get back to billet 4am.

Friday 7 July 1916

Lonely feeling all evening but pray to God for strength. Boys celebrate last evening before going to trenches. Sing 'Jesus, lover of my soul'.

Saturday 8 July 1916

7am hurry around and take blankets back to chateau. Good riddance to fleas ... trenches had a fearful banging about. Up to knees in slush and water and feel jolly tired. Bail water out almost hopeless job. Sleep for 2 hours like a log.[22]

Letters from wounded men were often printed in the press. They served a number of purposes. For one, they prepared the public for any future experience with an injured loved one. Moreover, as someone who had seen and suffered the consequences of war the views of an injured solider had gravitas.[23] Those who died could not speak, but the injured could and that meant they were the only ones who could offer the perspective of someone who had sacrificed, had paid dearly for doing their duty. This letter was published in the journal of the British Workers' League, an organisation that

Herbert Adams in 1916.
(Courtesy of Wirral
Archives, Y/P/X/27/6/3)

supported the war effort. The organisation returned seventeen National Democratic and Labour MPs in the 1918 election. Published some months before the United States of America entered the war, this letter cautions the British public against being too confident. Yet there is a defiant tone that turned out to be partly justified as British forces launched small-scale attacks on German positions in the winter of 1917, before being stalled on 17 February north of the Ancre River.

We have received from a correspondent the following letter from an invalidated soldier now lying in a military hospital in Liverpool, and publish it in order to show the indomitable spirit that is so characteristic of our fighting forces:

'I wonder what 1917 will bring for us? Has ever any year held such a puzzle for our country as the new one? Will it see the final triumph of our old Empire? It will not see its fall. Of that I am sure. Yet we should not enter into it in any swashbuckling spirit. We must be prepared to go on steadily and relentlessly, each of us doing his little bit for our common heritage and in justice to the glorious dead. We know that in years gone by our forebears bled and died and made our name one to be conjured with. But never have we spent so much of our best life, and when we emerge victorious and cleansed by the awful fires, how much greater it will be! I am not a proud man generally, but to call myself an Englishman is worth to me all I ever have to put up with ... Nobody likes war; it is awful and blasting, but *I do hope to be able to go out again soon and carry on, doing just what I should.* This is no time for personal sentiment. The man or woman who puts personal feelings before the Flag is not worthy. Also, if we should lose, although that is unthinkable, how much good would personal things be then? The men who said they should stay at home for this reason or that, how much could they do, think you, to save the women and children from the German cruelty and lust? For, to be sure, they would like nothing more than to run amok in our island. No, we've got to fight them out there and be as cold and merciless as we can. They have properly roused the Viking and Norman blood in us English and may we make them rue it.'[24]

The following account of a march from the magazine of the 6th Battalion Manchester Regiment while at camp in Southport gives an idea of the training that was undertaken at home before heading off to war. Long marches with full kit tested physical endurance and willpower. The rivalry between the different companies based in Southport provided an incentive, as did the reaction of the people who saw the soldiers march through the streets. This was not described as a recruiting march, yet the sight may have inspired men to sign up. From the description of the arduous journey back, however, some potential recruits may well have been put off.

Owing doubtless to the invigorating influence of spring, the battalion has been ravaged by an epidemic of record-breaking, and out of the dust of the conflict (after the figure) C Company has emerged victorious. The successful effort was made on April 19th and the feat accomplished was a march (carrying rifles and great coats) from Southport to Liverpool on the Birkdale, Formby, Great Crosby, Waterloo Road, and back the same way as far as Formby, the total distance being 35 miles. Two platoons (the old 9 and 12) took part in the march, Lieutenant Reiss being in command; and of the 97 men who started from Fisher Drive, 77 completed the full distance – an achievement of which the company is justifiably proud. One point deserving special mention is that eight men just fresh from the depot went on the march – their first parade in Southport! – and four of their number saw the thing through. The two hours' rest enjoyed at Liverpool (which was reached in less than 6 and a half hours) bucked up the men a good deal, and they were in good fettle when, soon after six o'clock, they started back. Seven miles on stone setts [paving] (from Liverpool landing-stage to Great Crosby) tried them very severely, however and most of them were all but 'shot' when Formby was reached, from which station the return to Southport was made by train. It is worthy of note that the march was sprung on the two platoons without any previous warning.[25]

Just as men went to war for all sorts of reasons, so there were many reasons why men did not join the Army. Some waited until they were conscripted. Others were exempt because they worked in reserve occupations or were unfit for military service. For those who could serve but did not want to, however, there was an opportunity to put their case before a military tribunal. Conscientious objectors, of whom one of the most well-known from Liverpool was Sydney Silverman, objected to war for a variety of religious or moral principles.[26] The first example below illustrates how ridicule and humour were deployed to undermine the objector's arguments. Employers could also attempt to ensure that their workers remained at their posts, even if they were eligible for service or did not work in the officially designated reserve occupations. In the second example, the treasurer of the Liverpool Seaman's Orphan Institution presents a case for a teacher not to be conscripted. The third example does not relate to a tribunal, but the accident victim's last words do indicate opposition to the call up. By 1918, measures were put in place to take some of the younger workers from reserve occupations. It was likely that the unfortunate John McGuire faced the prospect of serving at the front.

'What would you do,' asked the Lord Mayor at the sitting of the Liverpool County Tribunal, this afternoon, of a conscientious objector from Wigan, 'if the Germans came along to shoot your wife?'

'I would be like the ladies, Sir. I would ask them to sit down to a cup of tea.' (Laughter.)

'Do you mean to tell me that in all seriousness?' demanded the Lord Mayor.

'That, observed the appellant, would be defence in a different manner.'

'Is that your answer?' Inquired his lordship, to which the appellant replied, 'That is the answer I would give to that. I would not use physical force.'

'Is it your answer if a German came to attack your wife you would not use physical force, but instead you would ask him to sit down and have a cup of tea?'

'I would be friendly with him, and I would not use physical force,' was the reply.

'Do you want to get rid of your wife?' gravely inquired the Lord Mayor amidst laughter.

'I don't,' said the appellant.

The Lord Mayor, 'If a German came to shoot your wife she would be dead before the cup of tea were ready.' (Laughter.)

The appellant added that he objected as a Christian to taking the military oath.

The Lord Mayor pointed out that as a military service man he would not have to take the oath.

'So,' explained his lordship, 'your objection there has gone. That satisfies you, doesn't it?'

Appellant, 'I cannot take part in military service.'

Alderman Maxwell, 'It would give him a chance of giving the Germans a cup of tea in the trenches.'

Appellant said neither he nor any member of his family believed in the Army, and he was not reaping any benefit from the war.'

The appeal for exemption was dismissed, the Lord Mayor remarking that they would give the appellant an 'opportunity of giving the Germans a cup of tea.'[27]

Liverpool Seaman's Orphan Institution, 9 Oriel Chambers, 14 Water Street, Liverpool

Liverpool 15 August 1917

To the chairman of the tribunal for Liverpool.

Dear Sir,

On behalf of the committee of the above institution, I beg leave to appeal to your tribunal to allow Mr James Bell Jackson to remain at his present work as a house master and teacher.

The institution lost three of their staff early in the war, and recently a substitute, and now another has been called up.

The institution would suffer greatly were he to be taken from us, for it would be almost impossible now to find another suitable substitute for the important work of teaching and training our boys, and if our staff should be insufficient and the standard of work fell below the education inspector's requirement, the institution would be in danger of losing the government grant, a matter of some £400 a year, which would be a very serious thing for the charity.

I particularly wish to draw the attention of the tribunal to the fact that this institution is much more than a scholastic establishment, for it is the boy's home, in which they live until 14 years of age, and are entirely fed, clothed and cared for, so that it requires more than an ordinary scholastic teacher to fill the post satisfactorily, his duties moreover occupy his full time throughout the day, and he lives in the building, in case he should be required at night.

On these special grounds I beg to appeal to the tribunal to leave Mr Jackson where he now is, for he is most certainly doing good and important work for the nation.

Our chaplain, the Revd C. W. R. Higham, will appeal personally.

I am yours truly,

J. H. Beazley.[28]

Mr. Samuel Brighouse held an inquest at Bootle on Tuesday, concerning the death of John Thomas McGuire (18), a locomotive fireman who died at the Borough Hospital on Friday evening, as the result of injuries sustained at an Aintree factory earlier the same day. Deceased had lived with his parents at Long-lane, Aintree. On Friday, deceased was engaged with another youth in traffic operations on a local railway at the factory. He was using a coupling pole to press down the brake, and it was supposed he had pushed the latter too far and that it was caught by the wheels. The pole flew back, struck McGuire, and he was knocked on the rails, where a succeeding wagon went over him. When picked up badly injured, deceased said to a policeman who had seen him the previous day with regard to military service, 'You won't get me for the Army now.' He was taken to Bootle Hospital, where he died the same evening. A verdict of 'Death by misadventure' was returned, and the locomotive driver exonerated from all blame.[29]

No one was more aware of the strains placed on men who occupied important administrative positions during the war than their wives. After his death, James W. Alsop's wife Constance wrote a biography that traced her husband's contribution to education and the war effort. Alsop worked in the university, as president of the University Council between 1909 and 1918 and Pro-Chancellor from 1918 to 1921, and was also chairman of Liverpool City Council's Education Committee. This extract gives some idea of the pressures that the war and other commitments placed on leading civic figures such as Alsop. At the same time, it captures some of the optimism that came towards the end of the war as American troops arrived in Liverpool.

All this year, 1918, things at the front were extremely anxious, though it became gradually more certain that the 'Allies' were holding their own, but terrible things were happening, and the submarine warfare was at its height. On April 25th there was a very largely attended intercessory service held in the Liverpool Exchange News Room, and I remember James, with many other friends, going to it; and a little later on August 4th, Remembrance Day, we went over to a very wonderful open-air service held on Sunday in front of St. George's Hall, when ministers of many denominations took part, and the beloved Bishop Chavasse spoke to that great multitude. The feeling everywhere was intense. The strain of war seemed to have become almost unbearable, and yet no one gave in, but struggled to find every means possible of heartening each other as hope came slowly nearer ...

In May, James sent in his resignation of the Chairmanship of the Military Tribunal. The pressure of office and other work had become so great that he could no longer attend the meetings and do the work needed.

At this time the American troops were pouring over to England to give their help at the last to the exhausted countries of Europe. Many things were done to welcome these troops at the port of Liverpool, but too often, alas, the men were in those days received into hospital on their arrival, as a scourge of influenza and pneumonia fell upon the crowded ships that brought them over; but those of them who marched through our streets, and they were many, were received with glad welcome, and when it was possible to entertain them in public or give them welcome in private homes, it was gladly offered, and everyone rejoiced to see them come. I remember James often speaking to me with the deepest sympathy for them: passing, passing, passing down the streets with their jaunty air but sad faces, in a strange country, and on the way to a terrible war. We, too, with many others offered hospitality to them in our home, and took part in an evening reception in Liverpool to the officers of the American Army and Navy, and in July there was a great review of American troops, and a Town Hall luncheon to the officers.

By this time, Sir Alfred Dale was better, and back again at the University, but it was known that he was likely to send in his resignation before the end of the year, though it would not take effect until some months later; but it was such a grave prospect that those who had the University concerns at heart were already looking round for someone who, when the sad time came, could fill his place. All these discussions and anxieties fell heavily on James as President of the Council and Pro-Chancellor, and not only occupied time, but a great deal of thought, and the idea of losing Sir Alfred was depressing to him.[30]

What became known as the Second Battle of Ypres was the only major German offensive on the Western Front during 1915. To compensate for their relative lack of manpower, the Germans

The scholar and educationalist James W. Alsop. (Author's collection)

deployed chlorine gas. This was the first effective use of gas on a battlefield. Norman F. Ellison's account of the start of the battle focuses on the bombardment of the city and seeing the gas cloud envelop French forces. Later, in April 1915, Ellison, who was a member of the 6th Liverpool Rifles, sustained an injury. During 1917 he was invalided after suffering frostbite. His memoir paints a picture of destruction and mentions the plight of displaced civilians. In the Second World War, Ellison experienced a similar fate to those he saw in Ypres when he had to evacuate his home during a bombing raid on Liverpool. This account of a bombardment and gas attack deals with the horror of war but also celebrates the heroism of those who assisted the injured.

On the 19th April the second great bombardment of Ypres started. High above our heads we heard the passage, like the rumbling of a railway train, of enormous 17 inch howitzer shells. As they burst amongst the buildings of the town, reddish clouds of brickdust, hundreds of feet high, shot into the air and slowly expanded into a heavy pall over the doomed place. The damage caused by these large shells was enormous. A few weeks later I was with a party in Ypres looking for unbroken mirrors to cut up into periscopes. The streets were pocked with shell craters forty feet across and as many feet deep; whole rows of houses had collapsed like a pack of cards; many had the whole facade torn off to expose the interior floor by floor, like some tragic doll's house with a hinged front.

The bombardment had been expected and the battalion details in the town were ordered to find shelter. Our adjutant, whilst making enquiries about suitable cellars, was told of the great tunnels under the ramparts of the town, constructed some two hundred years before by the famous engineer Vauban, as powder magazines. These casements, the size of railway tunnels, were found filled with rubbish and apparently forgotten. We cleared them out and no better shelter could have been devised. The solid masonry and the depth of the covering earth made them practically shell-proof.

The first shell fell among a bunch of children at play and killed fifteen of them. Thereupon a panic ensued and terror stricken refugees, their few most precious belongings trundled upon a barrow, crowded into the bottle neck of the town and streamed along the Poperinge road – the only route to safety. Shells dropped amongst them. Terrible were the sights witnessed by the battalion details as under the untiring leadership of our Commanding Officer Major Graham Martin they organised search parties to help the wounded and dying in the streets, soldier and civilian alike. With wonderful courage, they worked day and night, each sortie from the casements a succession of narrow shaves.

The 22nd April was another spring day which had passed with a little intermittent shelling until about 5pm when suddenly the French 75s around Sanctuary road, a quarter mile to our left, commenced 'gun fire' for all they were worth. Our artillery joined in and presently the activity spread up the line to us. We were in the foremost point of the salient and looking backwards towards the French lines, we saw a cloud of greenish vapour slowly rolling over them. It was the first gas attack of the war, although at the time we did not know it.[31]

Olaf Stapledon's description of the destruction he saw about him during the war prefigure some of his later wolves of science fiction. As part of a Friends Ambulance Unit motor convoy, Stapledon experienced horrors that were far removed from his life as a Workers' Educational Association (WEA) tutor in Liverpool. His unit was stationed in the southern part of the Western Front, where there were very few British troops. The ambulance unit worked with the 16th Division of the French Army in Champagne, Argonne and Lorraine. The following extract starts with an account of Stapledon's second experience of combat and ends with a celebration at the end of the war. At Oxford in 1909, Stapledon had trained to be an officer. His decision not to take up a combatant role has been credited to his WEA students in Liverpool. Their questions about the war put a seed of doubt in his head that led to him becoming 'more and more sceptical of Britain's self-righteousness'.[32]

During the preliminary bombardment I spent a night in a certain dug-out with an English companion and a number of French 'brancardiers' [stretcher-bearers]. There was an almost continuous thud of shells overhead. Our French colleagues kept up an agitated conversation all night. I lay in a bunk trying to sleep, hoping there wouldn't be a call, and trembling so violently that the wire mattress creaked. Next morning it turned out that my companion had slept solidly and heard nothing of the bombardment.

The attack began, and once more we were all working night and day. As usual there was one particularly bad stretch of road, constantly shelled. It was here that I left a wounded man by the road-side. I was going up with an empty car. Shells were landing all round. One was near enough to shift the car sideways. In the ditch was a man with a smashed head, obviously dead. I drove on at top speed, crashing into shell holes. The next car that came along stopped during heavy shell-fire and picked him up. He was alive. That was a pretty bad mistake on my part, not easily forgotten …

A plague of flies gave us all 'trench fever,' and reduced our numbers to half the normal strength. Those who remained were always cursed with diarrhoea, and always dog-tired with the constant strain and work. Drivers sometimes fell asleep at the wheel. Roads at the front, of course, were very badly smashed. There was a good deal of gas; and gas-masks do not conduce to good driving, least of all at night. As something of a fresh-air fiend, I violently loathed sleeping behind a gas-proof curtain. Once, when no dug-out or cellar was available, some of us slept in an old pig-stye. In the morning some French engineers came to bury us, supposing us to be corpses.

As usual we were extraordinarily free from casualties. Only one of our remaining members was killed; but he, Colin Priestman, was one whom we could ill afford to lose.

The actual advance took place through devastated country over corduroy roads and pontoon bridges. The villages were all destroyed, some completely obliterated. Some were smouldering ruins. In one village we came upon a rough notice in German to the effect that the library must be treated with respect, since books are men's best friends. Of the library itself there was no trace.

A few days before the armistice our division was withdrawn. We retired to Ay. When the armistice was declared I was sent with a companion to raid the deserted wine-cellars of Reims for the convoy's armistice celebrations. We collected, if I remember rightly, about forty bottles of champagne, but before we had stowed them in the car, two 'flicks' (military gendarmes) appeared, and we had to retreat empty-handed and in haste. Fortunately the mayor of Ay presented the convoy with more than enough wine for its carousal. I hope the Friends will forgive me for recording this significant little incident which crowned the long and strange career of S.S.A. *[Section Sanitaire Anglaise]* 13.[33]

Three letters from troops who entered Jerusalem around Christmastime in 1918 were published in a Birkenhead newspaper. They are vivid accounts of a victory that attracted much interest at home and helped boost home front morale during a very difficult winter. Prime Minister David Lloyd George supported the case for a dynamic military operation in the Holy Land because it would be something very different from the deadlock on the Western Front. The conquest of Jerusalem and later action in the Middle East is not thought to have contributed to the capitulation of the Ottoman Empire. Indeed, the War Office did not think it of any significance. A German newspaper noted, 'This is doubtless a success for the English, though more moral than military ... the conqueror of the city, of course, gains a halo.'[34] Those who wrote these letters wore that halo. The soldiers were excited and knew that their readers were familiar with the city and some of its features. Many of the men would have read about Jerusalem as children. Now they were its liberators.

One of our local soldiers now serving with the Egyptian Expeditionary Force, writing to his friends in Neston, says:

'Jerusalem, Dec 27th. The Turkish attempt to take back Jerusalem this morning was a failure, and their dead are numbered thousands. They were new troops and the majority Germans, but our lads were ready for them. I shall never forget my Christmas out here as we were waiting in a heavy rainstorm at 5 a.m. on Christmas morning for the Turks, but later we went into billets, and were served with wine and cigarettes, the only extras which could be got up in time owing to transport difficulties. The plum pudding has not arrived, and all the mails are delayed, so we have to be satisfied with bully and biscuits. We came into billets in the town yesterday, and I hope things will quieten down a little so that we can stop here. It is a large monastery and a very comfortable place. I have plenty of money in my pocket, but it is not of much use as the 'Golden City' can't supply us with anything only oranges. The inhabitants were very glad to see the British for several reasons. This has been a very interesting big push, and what I would like to tell you in my letter must remain untold for the present. But I have been on the Mount of Olives, which is something to swank about. The pen and ink I am using now are what the Turks left behind them.'

The following extracts are taken from the letter of one who was attached to the first squadron to enter Jerusalem:

'When we entered the populace were mad with joy. There was great cheering and clapping of hands; also shouts of "You are welcome," etc., and old women and men crying with joy. People offered us wine, nuts, bread, and all sorts of things to eat but we had to get on towards the Jericho road, along which the Turks were retiring. The city was officially taken over at 3.30 the same afternoon. When we had reached the old walls at the other side of the town we were held up by the machine-guns and rifles of the Turks, who had taken up a position on the Mount of Olives ...'

Writing to his mother in Birkenhead, another local soldier says,

I expect you are wondering where I am. Well, at present I am at =, described in the 'Birkenhead News' as one of the most ancient of existing cities ... By jingo! We are having real Blighty weather. To start with wind and rain, then cold and dry, with a frost in the mornings, so we feel it a bit after the warm weather. Still, we were jolly glad to get rid of the fleas, which were a dreadful nuisance not long ago ... Thank father for sending the paper, also the Birkonian [Birkenhead School newsletter]. I have finished reading Lloyd George's fine speech at Paris; it certainly is a remarkable one, and he has a wonderful open way of stating a few facts.'[35]

Like many other volatile situations, wars breed superstition and supernatural encounters. Ghosts and messages from loved ones are part of the psychological landscape of war. 'The Angels of Mons' is the most common 'ghost story' of the conflict. This spectral spectacular was just one instance of the otherworldly paying a visit to the First World War. A study of Canadian soldiers during the war has shown how tales of encounters with the supernatural helped the troops make sense of their time at war.[36] Two kinds of ghost are identified in the following passage. The first is a vision of a dead soldier that terrifies a hefty Irishman from Liverpool. The second is a benign but unsettling visitation from the author's mother. Tommy Kehoe was the bugler for the 5th King's Liverpool Regiment who, in his account of the war, remarks that his bugling was so poor he was given a gun instead, and all at the age of sixteen. During the Second World War he was killed during the blitz on Merseyside on 3 May 1941.

There is something about night sentry-go that stirs up a lad's imagination till everything about him is like a dream, and mostly like a bad dream, too. The Irish boys from Liverpool are always seeing ghosts in the dark. Brannigan used to see a headless soldier walking up and down in front of the trench, and he would watch the thing until cold shivers ran through him. He saw the headless soldier coming for him in a raid once, and it was the only time I saw Big Tom afraid. He came near to getting shot by his officer for starting to run back to our trench. And one day a little later, when a Hun whose head had just been blown off tumbled right on top of him in a shell hole he let out a yell that we could hear above the artillery.

That first night on guard I saw something myself that I know now couldn't have been true but that I couldn't get out of my mind for days and days afterward. As I was staring over the top a rocket went up from the Germans and sent a broad path of light from their trench almost to ours. Right in the centre of that lighted way I saw somebody coming toward me. It was a woman with her arms stretched out, as if she were pleading. The light was shining full on her face, and I saw it was my mother.

I thought I heard her calling,

'Tommy, lad! Tommy, lad!'

But the artillery was going just then and I knew I couldn't have heard her voice at that distance.

Then the light went out and she disappeared in the dark.

I believed that night that I really had seen her, and I wondered whether she was groping about for me out there in the dark. Then I began to be afraid. I thought my mother might be dead and that this was her ghost come to find me. It was terrible to think of her moving about out there among all those dead men; but it seemed just as bad to have her creeping toward me out of the dark. Ghosts are ghosts, and I didn't care to meet with one alone in the night, even my mother's.

A week later I got a letter from her that told me she was as well as ever.

It wasn't death or the dead soldiers that frightened the Tommies; it was those dead solders' ghosts.[37]

While not all men who served were especially religious, religion did play a part in the lives of many soldiers. A large number of practising Catholics served in the British Army, and by the end of the war over 600 Catholic chaplains served their spiritual needs. In the following account, Father Corcoran is optimistic about the effect of the war on attitudes towards religion. He believed that the war would educate Protestants from all classes about Catholicism, rendering it less mysterious. Therefore something good could come out of the war. Corcoran was not the only chaplain to find inspiration in the Dardanelles. Indeed, the sight of so many men taking to prayer made many go further than Corcoran and claim to have witnessed a religious revival. Yet this optimism appears to have been relatively short-lived. Later in the war, many chaplains, both Protestant and Catholic, were sceptical about the extent to which prayer and religious observance at the front represented a sincere, substantial turn towards organised religion.[38]

On Sunday morning Fr Corcoran, who recently returned from the Dardanelles, where he had been acting as chaplain to the Catholic members of the British forces, paid a visit to the Sacred Heart Church, St Helens, and delivered an address on the work of Catholic chaplains at the front.

'At the first I was attached to a Border regiment with a great many Catholics,' said Fr Corcoran, and with them I went to the trenches and stayed there seeing the men fairly often. Later on I was at the landing at Sulva Bay, and I had four battalions. After a certain number of days they came down to rest trenches or a rest camp, though there is no such thing as rest in the East, but they were not in the firing line, and one could see them a great deal better.

'The men had every opportunity of attending to their duties before, perhaps, they were called before God. There was no shame about the practice of their religion; there was no shame about going to confession. When the Catholic soldier stepped out of the trench and stood in front of the priest the non-Catholic soldier knew he was going to confession. When the war is over, the idea of the confessional will not be such a secret business as it is to-day, and as it has been in the past among non-Catholics. Millions of men have seen Catholics going to confession openly, and the same with regard to Mass. Non-Catholics are all around, and they go on with their meals or whatever they are doing. They see the priests in their vestments, and all the time I was there I never saw any sign of disrespect to the priest.

'At times, one has to receive converts. One man came and said he wanted to be a Catholic. I explained the elements of our religion, and then with the water in his water bottle I baptised him. We have no churches, there is no shelter, and we say Mass in the open, sometimes in a dug-out, and on one occasion I said Mass in a hole a few feet deep. The communicants had to jump down into the hole to receive Holy Communion, and then jump out again.

'A curious thing happened at Hellas, where we had just landed. Our generals were afraid of massing the troops together for church services because we were well within range of the enemy's guns. On the Sunday I wanted to arrange Mass, and I went to the commanding general, but he said he did not think I could have permission. I happened to be talking to the officers of a French battery of artillery, and I obtained permission to say Mass for the French soldiers. Some of the officers could not understand how Mass could be said by an English priest for the French soldiers. Some of our men were under the same impression, but when they came back it helped them to understand the universality of the Church.'[39]

These letters were written by George Andrew Herdman to his parents and are included in a biography written by his father. His accounts provide an insight into the training that men experienced on the front as well as what they did in their leisure time. Herdman was born at Bentley Road, Liverpool, and joined the Officers' Training Corps after he went to Cambridge University in the autumn of 1914. He cut short his study of mathematics, physics and chemistry in order to join the 15th King's Liverpool Regiment at the start of 1915. Herdman had leave at the start of June and visited his parents in Liverpool and his sister in London before returning to the front where he fell on 1 July 1916 at the Battle of the Somme, aged twenty-one. At this point Herdman had been transferred to the 18th King's Battalion, a Pals rather than a territorial battalion like the 15th and the 7th.

23 March 1916.

We are billeted in a fair-sized village, and are at present employed on road clearing which is, I think, the most boring job I have ever come across, though it is very necessary as heavy transport makes an awful mess of the roads. I don't know how long we are here for, but there is no rumour of a move yet.

Football matches have been arranged between us and some other troops billeted in the same village. There is a YMCA hut here where they had a cinema show the other night.

27 March 1916.

[Picture postcard of ruined Cathedral with the name obliterated].

This is the cathedral in a town [Albert] a few miles from here. I went to see it the other day. The ground all round is pitted with shell-holes. Notice the extraordinary result of a shell striking the statue on the tower.

3 April 1916.

I have been detailed to attend an engineering course given by the RE [Royal Engineers] to some infantry officers and NCO's [*sic*]. I suppose they will teach us all about making trenches, dug-outs, wire entanglements, etc. I think it ought to be rather interesting. It is in a small town near here. I am going there this afternoon. It is to last for ten days to a fortnight.

Yesterday we had a demonstration with a German 'flammenwerfer' which was captured some time ago. It is the liquid flame machine. The object was to show that if you crouched down close to the parapet of the trench you were perfectly safe. Some of us were put in a trench and the flame turned on to the trench. It is like an enormous blow-lamp used by painters, and the flame is 20 to 30 yards long. It is very hot, but the flame does not go down into the trenches.

23 June 1916.

I reached the battalion on Wednesday morning at a place a good way behind the line (quite near where I was before [Amiens] with the 7th last December). All leave for officers has been stopped, so I was rather lucky to get mine when I did.

They adopted daylight saving here the night before last. Unfortunately, they didn't take the trouble to tell us they were going to do it beforehand, so most of us got up an hour late for breakfast.

To-day they put us all into a gas chamber with gas helmets on to show us that they gave complete protection. The gas was said to be several times stronger than that used in an attack. Of course breathing in the helmets was very uncomfortable, but no more so than in fresh air. The only sign of the presence of gas was that all our buttons went grey.[40]

William Banks died almost a year after George Herdman fell. William was listed as a farm labourer in the 1911 census and lived with his father, who was a widower, his grandmother, three uncles and his sister. Although his father, a general labourer, did not publish a biography like George Herdman's father, we can learn something about this ill-fated young man from letters that were sent to his family after his death by his section commander and two of his friends. The publication of such letters in the local press was not unusual. In this way, a family's grief could be made known to a wider circle of friends and acquaintances; or a son's heroism might be proclaimed to the locality. This account of an unexpected death after a fragment of a shell used to deliver poison gas wounded William's leg is a family tragedy that epitomises the fate of many others. Although gas did not play a conclusive role in battles during the war, its very nature and the need for those who were attacked to take precautions meant that the slightest errors or oversights could cost lives. Even those who survived could have their health affected for the rest of their lives.

The circumstances of the death of Gunner William Banks, Shore Cottage, Meols, are related in the following letter from his section

George Herdman fell on the first day of the Somme. (Author's collection)

commander (Second-Lieut T. W. B. Brodbell): 'I was very shocked and sorry this morning to hear of the death of your son, Gunner Banks, from gunshot wound and gas poisoning. I am afraid you will have already received the official intimation from the War Office, and wish I had sent you a few lines when your son was wounded. For several days we had been preparing for the offensive in front of Arras, and Saturday, 7th April, was a particularly busy one. I had been on duty early, and had been relieved for breakfast. Between 10 and 11 a.m., whilst I happened to be shaving, some gas shells began to come over. I did not take very much notice, as they seemed clear of us, but in the course of their 'sweeping and searching' the Huns sprinkled us in turn. The commanding officer had just come to where I was to get his respirator in case of emergency when the shells began to fall close – so close, in fact, that he was temporarily affected, and I had to go and take the men to a safe spot. On looking in the direction of the guns I found that one shell had also fallen close to No. 1 detachment in which your son was. Several of the gunners were affected by the gas. We got them away, and your son said his leg hurt him. There was 'a cut' about an inch and a half long, but not very deep, on his calf. As the shell had dropped amongst some bricks a few yards away from where he was we were in doubt as to whether a piece of brick had hit him. The wound did not appear to have been caused by a metal splinter. The doctor attached to our contingent was almost immediately on the spot, and attended to your son whom I saw and spoke to in a small dugout. He had his leg bandaged and did not seem in any pain, but just a little sickly from inhaling some of the fumes. I did not think he was at all badly hurt. His leg had swollen a little and the doctor said he would have to go to hospital. We all regarded the matter to be of so slight a character as to be hardly a wound as the term is ordinarily understood. Naturally, it did not occur to me, as his section officer, to write to you about the incident, as I fully expected he would communicate the news to you himself. I had quite a shock to-day on hearing that he died within 24 hours. There can be no doubt that your son had immediate and expert attention. Not being a doctor myself I can only assume that he must have been hit by the shell, and some of the poison thus passed into his leg and eventually into his system. I assume that had the doctor really known gas poison was in the wound, and know the result would be what, alas, we now know, he would have had the limb amputated straight away, and possibly that might have saved your son's life. At the same time, amputation is a serious matter, and should not be undertaken unless known to be necessary. You will understand I have only expressed my own ideas; I may be quite wrong. However, I thought you would like to know my own feeling about your son. I am very sorry about his death, and have felt a sense of your loss all day. Your son was most popular in the detachment. He was very reliable and was the 'No. 2' on the gun, his duty being to assist with the ramming operations. We shall all miss him very much indeed, and I wish there were many more like him to take his place in my detachment.' The writer of the letter proceeds to explain that he has taken steps to get fuller information, and concludes 'with most sincere sympathy and sorrow at your loss, which we all share.'

Two of the deceased's pals (Gunner J. Moss and J. Shelbourne) during the course of a sympathetic letter, reported that: 'Will did not think he was badly wounded, as he made quite light of it. He was a very willing lad and a good soldier. His smiling face and good companionship will be sadly missed by all the boys. You will have the deepest sympathy of all the battery in your sad bereavement.'[41]

Every death is a tragedy, but some acquire more significance than others. Perhaps the deceased had been awarded a posthumous medal. Or the dead soldier was the first to die from a family, street, village or an institution. The first to fall came to stand for the others that followed. Among students of Liverpool University, Stuart Kirby Jones had this unfortunate honour. This obituary in the student magazine provides some details about Jones's life and what others thought about him. The references to sacrifice and service were repeated in obituaries throughout the war. Like the more well-known Liverpool University graduate and double VC winner, Noel Chavasse, the veterinarian Jones was a medical man. The deaths of those who heal others, human or non-human, seem particularly poignant.

The first student of Liverpool University to sacrifice his life for the defence of his country's honour was Lieutenant Stuart Kirby Jones. He was wounded in what is known as 'the battle of the Aisne,' on September 15th, and succumbed to his wounds in hospital. He was buried at Versailles with full military honours on September 21st.

Lieut Kirby Jones who was 24 years of age, was a Veterinary Officer in charge of the 25th Brigade of the Royal Field Artillery. Leaving a splendid practice which he was building up in Pembroke, South Wales, he embarked with the 1st Expeditionary Force to France, and performed part of the brilliant work which the Army Veterinary Corps has done during the war. His fatal wounds were received in performing this humane though hazardous work.

Kirby, as he was known, was a general favourite at college. He had a genial and open disposition, which soon attracted a large circle of friends. His academic career was very successful, and culminated in an 'honours' final.

He was a keen athlete, and in 1909 carried off the 220 yards handicap at the sports. His athletic prowess was especially marked at the Liverpool Institute, where he received his preliminary education.

His brother Glyn Jones qualified recently as a dentist at this university.

We mourn the loss of a staunch friend, but rejoice that he died in so noble a cause as the defence of his country.[42]

In his poetry, Siegfried Sassoon evoked the landscapes of Sussex and Kent. His work, and that of other war poets, has been described as a 'recourse to the pastoral'.[43] When they evoked the countryside, poets used that landscape to signify the whole nation. While this is often seen as a romantic notion of England that leaves out the less aesthetically pleasing parts of the country, there is no doubt that a picturesque imagining of their home helped men get through the war. Although the following poem is not from the pen of any of those poets who are in the canon of Great War poetry, like some of the more renowned works it praises a particular English landscape. The poem illustrates the power of local identity in the minds of those who either fought or thought about the war.[44] For those in strange, foreign lands, where the scenery had been transformed by the fighting, images of familiar places provided some comfort.

Between the Mersey and the Dee.

There's an unconsidered corner
Of the distant Motherland,
Where the wild salt winds are blowing
On a shore of golden sand;
And behind the little sandhills lies
A kingdom of the sea;
And there's magic in the air between the Mersey and the Dee.

Oh, I long to see the sandhills,
And listen to the roar,
Of the Western sea that breaks upon
The lonely Leasowe shore.
And I'm thinking of the glory
Of the sunset on the sea,
From the little hills that lie between
The Mersey and the Dee.

There's a lonely little maid, with eyes
That laugh and weep and speak;
She's as wayward as the winds that fan
The roses on her cheek.
But she's true and sweet and tender,
And her spirit's calling me,
From the little hills that lie between
The Mersey and the Dee.

G.D.W.[45]

The importance of local identity is also illustrated in this account of the work of the Liverpool Merchants' Mobile Hospital. War is commonly seen as a time of disturbance as people leave their homes and workplaces, some never to return. Yet in the midst of the dislocation, soldiers and others managed to maintain links with home. According to the British Medical Journal in 1915, the forty-five nurses and forty orderlies who staffed the hospital were 'all Liverpool people'.[46] By January 1915, a total of £25,000 in subscriptions for the hospital had been raised from Merseyside. Before the hospital left for continental Europe, the buildings were displayed in Ullet Road playground, guarded by a consignment of Pals. Among the many wounded treated at the hospital was C. S. Lewis, who was injured at Arras in April 1918. Examples like this suggest that alongside their national identities, soldiers had 'local loyalties': they were fighting for their home as well as their country.[47]

Where so many thousands of men were passing through a camp, there were sure to be some remarkable meetings and coincidences. Relations, who had not met for years before the war, might find themselves in the same ward, though one might have come from England and the other from Canada, Australia or New Zealand. Several times were brothers in the hospital at the same time, and from different regiments and fronts. We always took special interest and made special enquiries with regard to men from Lancashire and particularly Liverpool, and it was not uncommon to find relations and friends of our male and female staffs. Fathers, brothers and chums of one our VAD [Voluntary Aid Detachment] orderlies, sisters or medical officers, came in as patients, or as visitors who were passing through. In the convoy some grimy mud-covered individual might call out: 'Hullo, Doc!' or ask for one of the sisters. In our very first convoy the writer was making the routine enquiries as to name and age, and a young fellow replied: 'Well you ought to know, as you ushered me into the world.' Occasionally a wounded man would catch sight of the Liver design at the front of the hospital, or the title 'Liverpool' on our big Red Cross on the lawn, and would say: 'Good old Liverpool,' and grin with delight at finding a home from home.

Born in 1890 at Great Crosby, James Fitzmaurice was the son of a chief station porter who later became stationmaster at Waterloo. Unlike his father, James decided to find work abroad. After arriving in Western Australia he became a farm labourer and, at the outbreak of war, joined the 10th Light Horse. He was interviewed by Peter Liddle of Sunderland Polytechnic in 1974 and the extracts from the transcript below deal with his experience at Gallipoli in the offensive of August 1915. Like the attack on Jerusalem, some thought the Gallipoli offensive was a waste of resources that would have been better deployed elsewhere. Unlike Jerusalem, the controversy over Gallipoli has grown over the years. The casualties and evacuation of the troops after eight months left a bitter taste in the mouths of many, especially the colonial troops. Towards the end of the extract Liddle tries to find out what James felt after the assault failed. His simple response, some sixty years after the event, refers to a telling silence.

James Fitzmaurice (JF): I could not see much prospect of staying in England. I read the paper and was interested in Canada, Australia, New Zealand and hearing and reading I felt that Australia with its sunny climate would suit me nicely.

Peter Liddle (PL): Would the August offensive be one of your most vivid recollections of your service at Gallipoli?

JF: August 7 was something I couldn't tell you much about for the simple reason that I went over. Two lines of 12 before us. First line had fallen before us. I was in the second line and we got no order to advance. Nobody could see anything in front of you not a thing with the machine gun bullets stirring up the dust and you couldn't see anything. All I can tell you about August 7 we had to stay there until we got the order to retire and we lost quite a number retiring.

PL: Did you go over the top then?

JF: Over the top in the second line.

PL: But I thought nearly all were killed?

JF: Oh no.

PL: Opposite where were you, opposite which particular point?

JF: Right in the neck.

PL: And you were in that second line when all the accounts I have read have suggested that the second line as well as the first line were almost entirely killed?

JF: Well, it was an irregular line. I don't know. I might be wrong.

PL: You weren't touched?

JF: No. I was not touched.

PL: How far did you get?

JF: I would not say any more than about 20 or 30 yards but if you lifted your head at all you would have got it.

PL: Then you went to ground?

JF: Went to ground and kept your nose to the ground and never moved. I didn't.

PL: Regardless of what anybody was doing on either side?

JF: You couldn't. You were just waiting for orders, listening.

PL: And you heard no order to go to ground?

JF: Oh yes, as soon as we went over we went to ground and as I have said before about 18 yards. It wouldn't be any more.

PL: And how long did you have to remain there?

JF: We were there for at least half an hour to three quarters of an hour.

PL: And then?

JF: And then we got the order to retire. That came passed along the line several times and we retired with our noses still to the ground and fell back into our trenches.

PL: Facing which way?

JF: We turned round on our bellies and crawled back. I kept my nose that close to the ground, you couldn't get any closer.

PL: And you were being absolutely fired on all the time?

JF: Yes, absolutely.

PL: How did they miss you?

JF: Well, we were fortunate, we were in a little depression ... if you put your head up you would have been gone but we were a bit fortunate. Well, we must have been fortunate because about 80 of us came back out of the whole regiment. So a man must have been fortunate but it was a depression.

PL: Was the impact of this unsuccessful attack, this apparently suicidal attack in which so many men who by this time with varying degrees of closeness real friends of yours, was this a terribly scaring experience or could it accept it as just the way things went, fate?

JF: Well, of course, it is all very well to say that you go and do a job. Your instructions are to do this, that and the other but on reflection when you come back and think what an impossible job it was and you come to the conclusion we must have been there for a purpose and that was ...

PL: But when the roll was called some time later in the evening and so many people who had been there the previous evening were not there then, what sort of effect did this have on you?

JF: We hardly spoke to one another. We were so tired and we were so disappointed at not getting somewhere.[48]

Tales of escape from Germany, though doubtlessly embellished by escapees, gripped the public imagination.[49] The three escape attempts by Liverpool-born Lieutenant Walter Duncan of the 1/8th Liverpool Irish are recorded in his book *How I Escaped Germany*, which was published a year after his death from heart failure in 1918. After he returned from the camp in Ludwigshafen, on the other side of the Rhine from Mannheim, Duncan was received by the king and granted three months leave before taking up an intelligence post in Birmingham. In these excerpts from the final chapter of his book, Duncan describes his movements after having smuggled himself out of the camp in a large packing case. His previous unsuccessful attempts to escape from Augustabad and Ingolstadt had respectively involved tunnelling and filing through iron bars.

I walked at a smart pace to appear natural, through Ludwigshafen, to the big bridge across the Rhine, to Mannheim. The roads and the bridge were full of the usual Sunday afternoon crowds, but, walking naturally, I was not spoken to. I reached Mannheim about 5.15 pm, having, consequently, plenty of time for my train – the 6.54pm for Frankfurt. The route I planned was from Mannheim to Frankfurt, Frankfurt to Cologne, and Cologne to Aachen ...

Arrived at Mannheim my next problem was to find the main railway station. I knew it must be on some tram route, but I followed the tram lines in road after road in various directions without either reaching the station or seeing a tram bearing the words 'Haupt Bahnhof.' I singled out a man of unintelligent appearance, and asked him the way to the station, one of my stock questions which I had learnt from my teacher at Ludwigshafen. He repeated 'Haupt Bahnhof,' and I answered 'Oui,' but immediately seeing my mistake blurred it into a 'Ja, Ja,' and he did not notice my slip. I only partly understood his directions, but followed the way he pointed, and soon saw the tram I was looking for, with the sign 'Haupt Bahnhof' ...

First, I went to the bookstall, where after picking up and glancing through a number of novels, which I could not read, I bought one, and an illustrated paper ... I chose second-class as being the class in which I was least likely to be spoken to, my clothes being sufficiently good for that class. I went by a slow train in preference to a fast corridor train, partly to avoid the necessary conversation in paying the extra fare charged for the latter, but mainly because from the experience of other officers I had learnt that identification papers are more frequently examined on fast trains, the slow trains not being corridor trains, and it thus being impossible for an official to walk through the train on the journey. On showing my ticket at the barrier the collector told me the platform, and I found the train without difficulty.

I chose a non-smoking carriage, to avoid conversation about matches and cigarettes, etc. There was one man in the compartment, but I sat in a corner seat, pretending to read my paper and book, and he did not speak to me.

After two stations, this man went out, and for three stations I was alone, and took that opportunity of having some food. Then the door opened, and the only girl of attractive appearance I ever saw in Germany looked in. She asked me if the train was for Frankfurt, to which I replied, 'Ja.' She entered, and asked if she would have to change, and I, though not too certain replied, 'Nein,' and went on with my book. After a few minutes, she said something to me, the only word of which I understood being 'umsteigen' (to change). I tried to answer that the ticket collector had told me we did not change, but after three or four words, I stuck. I smiled at her, and she smiled back, and asked if I were going to Frankfurt, and on my answering 'Ja,' she said nothing further. She certainly saw I was a foreigner, but probably took me for a Dutchman.[50]

Aeroplanes often feature in the memoirs, diaries and letters of soldiers and sailors. Aircraft posed both a threat and a spectacle that many had never seen before. In a war that was frequently described using the language of chivalry and heroism, pilots were the knights of the air. Lieutenant Gilbert William Roger Mapplebeck, who was born in 34 Rodney Street in 1892, was an aerial Lancelot.

Walter Duncan – an experienced escapee. (Author's collection)

Not only was he the youngest squadron commander in the Royal Flying Corps, he was said to be the first to carry out an aerial reconnaissance of German territory in August 1914 and the first to bomb the enemy from the air. It was on one of these bombing raids in March 1915 when Mapplebeck, along with two other pilots, all flying BE2s, added another chapter to his adventures. After coming down near Lille, Mapplebeck travelled to Holland disguised as a French peasant. By the middle of April he was back in Britain. Yet within a few months he had died, after his plane crashed during a practice flight in England on 24 August 1915. His brother Tom was also a renowned pilot. The following items of correspondence relate to his escapades in March and April of 1915.

13 March 1915

Charles Longcroft (CL) to Sara Helen Mapplebeck (SHM)

I am afraid before you get this you will have seen in the papers that your son is missing. I did not write to you before as I have been expecting him to turn up at any moment.

He and 2 other officers of my squadron were taking part in a night raid last Thursday and your son and one of the other officers have not been heard of since. A thick mist got up soon after they started so I am very much afraid they must have got lost in the mist.

There have been several cases of officers getting back through the lines without being captured so I still live in hopes [*sic*] of his turning up again soon, but of course I have no absolutely no idea as to what has actually happened. One thing I am certain of is that, whatever happened could not have been avoided by skilful piloting as he is one of the finest pilots in the Corps ...

23 March 1915

CL to SHM

Before you get this you will have heard by wire that Gilbert is all right. I am sending this over however by King's Messenger to make certain that you get details.

Gilbert's engine gave out near Lille and he was forced to land and taken prisoner, so I'm afraid he won't be seen again until the end of the war but according to the report he is in excellent health and quite uninjured.

I cannot tell you how glad I am to be able to send you good news of him. He is a splendid fellow and has done splendid work in the Corps. I shall miss him terribly as he is one of the very best pilots and is a real good fellow in every way.

Undated

Gilbert William Mapplebeck (GWM) to SHM

My dearest mother – I am at present in Lille and am in good health. I hope to see you all again soon. Love to Neb and Monica and all my friends. Gib.

2 April 1915

GWM to SHM (scrap of cardboard, probably part of a postcard, printed in The Hague. Reverse has bottom of photograph with caption *Elisabeth Reine des Belges* [Elizabeth Queen of the Belgians])

Have escaped from Lille and am returning to England. I thought perhaps you might like to receive this. G.M.

3 April 1915

Major Hugh Hutchinson to SHM

I'll do what I can to get your note through to your son. My friend stipulated that he should not appear in any way in the matter, so I am afraid it would be impossible for you to see him. He has not yet returned from Paris.

I gave my information to the War Office and impressed on them the necessity of secrecy. Don't bother about the posting of your son as a prisoner. I think it is done to put the Germans off the scent and to cover my friend who gave me the information ...

6 April 1915 GWM to SHM

I have seen Major Hutchinson. He is very kind. I am going to see Lord Kitchener to-morrow in the afternoon and hope to get to Liverpool on Thursday ...[51]

The First World War did not involve as many sea battles as some had expected. This is not to say, however, that the war at sea was of little concern. During the Edwardian era, the public had followed the naval arms race between Britain and Germany as each nation strove to outdo its rival by building larger, more powerful 'castles of steel'. When the next 'great war' was discussed there were concerns about the effect it would have on trade. Many people on Merseyside also had family members who served in either the Royal Navy or the Merchant Navy. As these two accounts from stokers show, the experiences of those who served at sea provided some gripping stories. Stokers, also known as firemen, were responsible for maintaining the ship's fuel supply. Their role, at the heart of the ship, made their accounts all the more exciting for readers. The second account reveals how the press were eager to extract information from those who returned on leave.

Stoker William P. Reece, late of HMS. *Majestic*, and now on furlough at 45 Ireland Street, Halton View, tells an interesting story of the sinking of the ship in the Dardanelles. Before mobilisation, he was a postman in Widnes and had served 12 years in the Navy. On Tuesday he described to a *Weekly News* representative the last scenes on the ill-fated *Majestic*.

'She was sunk,' he said, 'early one morning. On board at the time were Rear-Admiral Nicholson, also a military general, who was wounded in the hand in the fighting on land, and Mr. Ashmead Bartlett, the official war correspondent. Rear-Admiral Nicholson was just setting out on a visit round the fleet.

'It was a sensation,' said Stoker Reece, 'I shall never forget. I had just been down the boilers, and came up to my mess to fry some bacon and have a real good breakfast. It was the first time we had bacon since Christmas. But I got no breakfast. You would have a job to describe the scene. We were so many times under shell fire, I thought it was a shell that had struck us. The shock, however, was out of the ordinary, and the ship seemed to split open and close again. When the crew started making for the upper decks we all had to go for ourselves. Every man – admiral and all – had to go into the water. The majority of men had life-saving belts on, but the one I had had been melted with the heat of the stoke hole. So I had to trust to having a strong nerve.

As I was making for the back of the ship I had to avoid the falling wood and things. When I got to the quarter deck I looked over the side and saw about 400 men in the water. I went round to the stern and five feet below I saw a chap in the water clinging to a chair. I dived over the side, and when I came up I clung to the chair, but the suction of the sinking vessel caught me and I had to let go. When the ship had almost turned over I tried to swim away, but could not for the suction. I think then when the ship took her final plunge the water threw me away from her. After swimming about 30 or 40 yards something pulled me down by the feet. I think I was pulled down twice, and I lost consciousness. When I came to myself I started swimming to a French trawler, and with the help of a rope I helped to save two other men. When I was picked up I had been about 30 minutes in the water, and they had to carry me aboard the trawler. Then I travelled about 100 miles with nothing but a blanket around me. We arrived in Plymouth on the 12th June.'

Stoker Reece has been about 89 times in action and at one time his ship was engaged in a bombardment for 25 days at a stretch. The Turks, he said, are very bad gunners, and if he were to put the British gunner in their place not a ship would enter the Straits.[52]

Another Hoylake sailor, and one who enjoys a great popularity in the district, has obtained a few days' leave in which to visit his numerous relatives and friends. Stoker George Bevan of 24, School-Lane presents a distinctly smart appearance as he parades Market-street in his uniform of blue. He is somewhat reticent about his thrilling experiences being of the type of lad who would endure almost anything rather than disclose information to the detriment of our cause. However, after a little persuasion he admitted having taken part in the North Sea battle when the *Blucher* was sent to her doom, and his ship was one of the convoy of destroyers which escorted the damaged flagship, *Lion* out of the danger zone. Stoker Bevan also mentions having recently paid a visit to Bedford, where the 4th Cheshires are stationed. He has seen quite a number of Hoylake lads, and declares that they look the very picture of health.[53]

Some who were overlooked for military service were determined to get into a uniform. Foremost among them were those who fell below the minimum height requirement. The press contains frequent references to men under 5' 3" who walked from recruiting station to recruiting station in a vain attempt to enlist. As the flow of eager, eligible recruits declined, the prospect of admitting short but healthy men did not seem so ridiculous. To maintain standards, however, prospective Bantams had to have a chest measurement of 33 inches or above. This was an inch above the minimum requirement for taller soldiers. The first Bantam regiments were raised by Birkenhead MP Alfred Bigland. Despite being a Quaker, the Conservative and Unionist politician was one of the most enthusiastic supporters of the war. One of those who joined the 15th Cheshire Bantam Battalion was Edward Hillison, a diminutive clerical worker from Liverpool. He became an orderly room sergeant and it was while he held this position that Hillison played a part in suppressing the mutiny at Etaples in September 1917. He describes this in an interview conducted in 1987.

Interviewer (Int): Where were you brought up, Mr Hillison?

Edward Hillison (EH): Brought up in Liverpool. My father was a hairdresser. He was an itinerant hairdresser. That is to say, he had a business in Liverpool, he had two actually – one a very good business on the main street in Liverpool, Lime street ... He also went on ships ... and he did pretty well out of that.

Int: What was life like in Liverpool in those days?

EH: It depended on what section of society you belonged to ... we were in the lower class but we graduated ... I tried to get into the army. I went down to the recruiting office. They wouldn't let me in of course.

Int: Could you just tell me what your reactions were to the outbreak of war?

EH: Similar to the other people I knew: indignation against the Germans ...

Int: How did you feel about not being able to enlist?

EH: I felt very indignant and I joined a volunteer thing, an amateur volunteer thing and drilled in the park and all that kind of thing with broomsticks in Sefton Park, Liverpool ... Anyhow, a man called Bigland who was the MP for Birkenhead ... He realised the situation that there were quite a lot of men who were short, there was nothing the matter with them at all, they were short that's all ...

Int: How did you hear about this 15th Battalion? [he later joined the 17th]

EH: I heard about it when I went around to the recruiting office. I kept in touch with the recruiting office. And to this day I can remember the recruiter's name he was an Army captain, Captain Frazer, Scotsman ...

Int: Did you witness any drilling [at Etaples].

EH: I saw some of the drilling going on and so forth. A lot of loud mouthed types used to march these fellows up and down and say nasty things about them. I did very little in the way of drilling myself. I was staff sergeant ...

Int: You were saying you were there when the mutiny occurred.

EH: In Etaples. While I was there this mutiny occurred. In retrospect you learned what it was. I did not know what it was. I know some chaps acted daft [they] marched down to, I think, a railway bridge or a bridge over a canal, I've forgotten which and started chucking things about and so forth. Didn't think a great deal of it.

Int: How did you hear about the rebellion?

EH: I was given a bunch, a small detachment of men to take down the bridge too but I didn't throw anything at anybody.

INT: What were you told to do at the bridge?

EH: Just to be there and resist these chaps, some were mutinying see? But ...

Int: Were they trying to get back into the camp?

EH: The men? Which ones do you mean, the rioters? No, I'm not sure, I think some of them had been denied leave or something and wanted to make a row. But it was all over fairly quickly. It was blown up quite a lot. But that kind of thing, it wasn't the only place you know that kind of thing happend. But Etaples became known. I only learned about it in that sense afterwards although I was in it to that extent.

Int: What incidents did you witness when you were down at the bridge with your detachment?

EH: I can't remember any particular incidents. It was all a bit of a melee. You just told them to stop that, put that down, pick that up, get over there, that kind of thing you see?

Int: And how did they react to your discipline?

EH: I can't tell you the language some of them used (laughs) But they didn't like sergeants anyhow. Men who were not sergeants didn't like sergeants. And little sergeants worse still.[54]

Food provides energy, but it does more than just fuel our bodies. Some foods can soothe a troubled mind, while others cause discomfort. Diaries and other sources show that soldiers often had food on their mind. Food was one way to help soldiers evoke memories of home. In 1916 the average daily ration for soldiers was 4,300 calories.[55] Yet, as indicated in the letter below, this did not always satisfy the tastebuds. Not every soldier, however, was fortunate enough to receive food from home. There were significant class differences and this could breed resentment.[56] This letter was penned by Arthur Behrend, who served as a platoon commander

The Bantams outside St George's Hall, Liverpool, 24 February 1915. (Author's collection)

at Gallipoli. While he may not have been ordering hampers from Fortnum and Mason, this member of a wealthy ship-owning family was able request some alternatives to the ubiquitous bully beef and hardtack biscuits.

Dear Hoyle

Would you be kind enough to buy me the following things and send me the amount whereupon I will send you a cheque on the Anglo-Egyptian Bank.

A soft field service cap, such as can be bought at Davies Bryans such as the regular officers of the 29th Durham bought. (Helmets are quite useless here) Size 71/8

4 tins of milk (unsweetened, small size)

4 tins of butter (1/2lb if possible)

6 tins of sardines

2 'Ever Ready' flashlight refills for ordinary pocket flashlight

A packet of candles

Some Velma or Petene chocolate (2/6d)

Have the whole packed in a wooden box as strongly as possible and if it weighs more than 10lbs, reduce the quantity of 2, 3 and 4 to suit.

I hope you don't mind the trouble but bully beef, milkless tea and biscuits get a trifle monotonous!

Second spasm (I've not finished yet)! 10 days later will you please send me 4 tins of milk, 2lbs of butter in 1/2 lb tins.[57]

2

Women and the War

The radical suffragette movement the Women's Social and Political Union (WSPU) suspended their campaign for the vote during the war. Emmeline Pankhurst, the WSPU's leader, and her daughter Christabel transferred their hostility from the male-dominated British political system to the militaristic 'male nation' of Germany.[1] This did not mean that the organisation's leaders were silent, however. By showing her patriotism Emmeline demonstrated that women could be better citizens than some men. The argument was: if an unpatriotic, possibly dangerous man has the vote why shouldn't a patriotic woman possess that right too? During her speech, Pankhurst criticises the more radical members of the Amalgamated Society of Engineers, who were currently engaged in an industrial dispute, and she is heckled by opponents of the continuation of the war. It was far from quiet on the home front when Pankhurst took to the stage. Her call for 'War till Victory' did not go down well among the war-weary.

Speaking at a crowded meeting at the Central Hall, Liverpool, Mrs Pankhurst declared that politicians had not always remembered the party truce, and the workers had struck, but the women had kept faith from the beginning. Considering the record of women in this war and their fidelity to their word, was there anything to fear from their getting a measure of political power, and from their bringing their qualities of directness and self-sacrifice into politics? She hoped that women would help to save the situation, and there was a situation indeed to be saved. At the front there were dangers, but the most dangerous front was at home, in the munition and aeroplane factories, and in the very hearts of the people. Russia was not only no use to us, but was a terrible danger, and yet there were people who were actually talking about and wanting revolution in England.

Some interruptions occurred when Mrs Pankhurst approached the question of the engineers, and there was a stream of interjections, some of them pacifist in sentiment and some directed rather irrelevantly against the profiteers. The speaker, who answered them with some effect, and with whom the vast majority of the audience were in sympathy, asked the older engineers whether they were going to allow these young men, who were hot-headed only to save their skins, to shelter in their organisation. She had herself fought against tyranny in the past, and she was prepared to take up the fight once more against a new form of class tyranny which tried to impose its will on the country. If, she declared, amidst applause, these autocrats of Labour would come out on strike for better conditions for mothers she would like them much better. Never had Socialism had such an opportunity as it had during the war, but it had been unsuccessful and become discredited, and discredited by reason of its pacifism and pro-Germanism.[2]

Catherine Morris was born in 1900 and lived with her mother and five sisters. As she was the eldest, she shared much of the burden of keeping house and looking after her siblings. Despite gaining a scholarship to Wallasey Grammar School, her mother told her to put her family first and stay at home. There may have been no male breadwinner in the Morris household, but the war provided employment opportunities for the whole family. Morris benefitted from a significant shift in the fortunes of women as they took on work that had previously been carried out by men. By the end of the war 4,808,800 women were in employment, an increase of more than one and a half million. Despite her comment about female train drivers, that role remained a male preserve.[3] Morris's reference to the new dress is significant because that item of clothing marked a very personal break from the past and a step up the social ladder.

During those four years women changed. Men were at war. So who were left? The women. Women took over the country, kept it going. Women were running businesses, driving trains. They made an amazing discovery, their independence. We realised that we didn't need men to guard us any more. We were just as able to do as much as they could. We were their equals. When the war was on, our family all worked together. Making bombs was our job. We did that for four years. Our family made quite a bit of money, all four of us and all working. Our income was quite a lot. We were wealthier than we used to be. For the first time I could buy myself a new dress. And 1918 was a breakthrough for women's rights. Women over the age of thirty could vote. It wasn't the same legal voting age as the man, but it was better than nothing. The suffragettes had claimed a victory![4]

Catherine Thornton (*née* Roach) was fifteen years older than Catherine Morris. Her mother died when she was thirteen and she brought up her younger brothers. Although their lives were very different, both of their recollections concern the experiences of working class women. Thornton held a variety of jobs, and her story illustrates how difficult it is to know for certain what people did for a living as the census only provides a snapshot once every ten years. Her comment about being unsuited to work as a coal heaver during the First World War does not fit well with common images of women happily taking up 'men's work'. Like her mother, Thornton appears to have been more suited for entrepreneurial activities than and labour. This account was provided by her grandson, Robert Faragher, in response to a call for information for an exhibition on women to be held at Liverpool library in 1989. If he had not responded, we would never have heard about this warm-hearted woman with a business head.

I was born in Liverpool in 1885. My mother ran a small general shop near to West Derby Road. I lived there with my 2 brothers. My father left us when I was little and went to work in Canada. He worked on the Canadian Pacific Railway and never really kept in touch. Times were pretty hard for most working class people and like most my mother couldn't wait for us to be earning ...

She [her mother] died of pneumonia when I was about 13. I tried to keep the shop going but I wasn't really up to it so I had to find a job. I got one working in a laundry in West Derby Road run by a Chinaman ...

I got a job after this working as an 'Officer' in the Belmont Workhouse. We did a lot of the laundry for the hospital and most of it was pretty dirty ...

I had to give reports on the women who worked there. A lot of them were mental. Sometimes they would go funny and you had to get to know when. If I saw them going funny I'd say 'let's stop for a bit and have a cup of tea'. Then I'd suggest they went and complained to the doctor and they'd get taken off till they were better ...

We worked long hours. I remember my younger brother Frankie complaining that there was never a hot meal for him when he came in. I got some horse manure and put it in a bowl and put it in the oven, I lit the fire and left a note saying there would be something different and hot for his meal when he got in that night. He got in and took the bowl of horse manure from the oven. Well it was hot and it was different ...

One of the women in the workhouse was there because she had had an illegitimate child and she stayed there for the rest of her life. She wasn't mental or anything. After the war she used to come round to see me because they were allowed out once a month and I used to give her 2*d* to go to the pictures ...

When the war started I got a job as a coal heaver but only stuck it for a short time. It was too hard. I then got a job in a munitions factory loading shells and near the end of the war dropped a box of them on my foot and broke all my toes. I decided to try and make a go of things by starting up a credit draper business. My mother had started up by hawking rabbits and hares round the posh parts of Liverpool but I was able to use my own money and borrow 20 sovereigns. You would sell a shirt for 2/11*d* or a pair of shoes for 3/6*d*. If you were lucky you would sell a man's suit for thirty bob. Some of the customers would borrow money too. I did quite well and bought a coal yard too. A cripple called Lame Sinott used to work for me. He used to take quarters of coal (28lb) from door to door. Often he'd fall over loading up and everyone thought that was a laugh.[5]

Charity was a prominent feature of the war on the home front. Giving time, money or items enabled people to feel that they were doing their bit for the war effort. These philanthropic actions build

Delivering coal on Tithebarn Street on 3 May 1918. (Courtesy of Liverpool Record Office, Liverpool Libraries 352 ENG/2/3311)

on a tradition of giving that had developed during the Victorian era as a result of urban problems and other social concerns. Women were often important figures in philanthropic endeavours and the following extract from the report of the Liverpool Civic Service League shows the role played by women in collecting and sorting donated material. The Civic Service League had been established during the Transport Strike of 1911 and soon set up a ladies branch. When war broke out, the League faced a new challenge. But it was not alone. The Women's War Service Bureau, founded by Dr Mary Birrell Davies and supported by Mayoress Rathbone, carried out similar activities. For a time there was some overlap and consequent tension between the two organisations.[6]

[T]he work of the League, in the collection and distribution of goods for the Forces grew so much during the first few weeks of the War that the limited accommodation in Exchange Buildings became far too small for the purpose …

By the kindness of Messrs. Robert Roberts & Co., Ltd., they [the committee] were able to secure the tenancy, rent free, of rooms on the ground floor of No. 30 Bold Street.

This Depot was opened on the 17th October last, and large quantities of used clothes began to arrive. The wide and general response to the appeal for such clothes has been remarkable. The mansion and the cottage have alike furnished contributions, in many cases of very superior quality and in excellent condition. Contributions of new garments, etc., have also been made by all classes. Ladies, working individually or in parties, have done much, and Political Associations have been constant contributors. Shop Assistants and Café Waitresses have filled in their spare time in knitting Socks, Mufflers, and Jackets for the League, and a surprising amount of work has been done by the Teachers and Pupils in the Schools. In some cases the League has provided materials, to be made up by the children in the Elementary Schools who could provide them themselves. Among the articles of used clothing dealt with at Bold Street are Suits of clothes, Overcoats, Caps, Clothing for Women and Children, Boots, Slippers, and Underclothing of all kinds. Walking Sticks, Pipes, and many other miscellaneous articles are also received in large numbers. Even perambulators and cots have been sent. The clothing for women and children has been chiefly sent to Belgian Refugees, for whom was also obtained a large quantity of Furniture, Tables, Pillows, Chairs, Ironmongery, China, and other household articles. A considerable amount of food has also been collected and sent to the Refugees.

Besides used clothing, a very large number of new articles have been received, including Blankets, Shirts, Cardigan Jackets, Mufflers, Socks, Mittens, Sweaters, Helmets, Belts, Kneecaps, Hose, Socks, Woollen Goods of all kinds, women and children's Clothing, Vaseline, Boracic Acid, Notepaper, Envelopes, Pencils, Soap, Books, Magazines, etc.

Through the generosity of Sir Benjamin Johnson, a considerable number of white sweaters have been dyed khaki colour and issued to the Troops, and many garments have been cleaned.

A great many articles used in hospitals have also been collected and distributed, such as Bandages, Sheets, Bed Jackets, Crutches, Bed Rests, Bed Socks, and Hospital Shirts ...

The used clothes are mainly required for soldiers arriving at and leaving the hospitals, as in a great many cases their uniforms are so soiled and torn as to be useless, and they require proper clothing until they can obtain new uniforms on rejoining the Forces after their recovery. Some of the used clothes collected are, however, too much worn to be useful for this purpose, and these are distributed to those in need of them in Liverpool, in some cases at the request of the senders. As a rule the recipients are soldiers' or sailors' wives, or the families of those out of work owing to the War.[7]

Being a female tram conductor was no easy ride. It was a very public role and often drew unwelcome attention. There were also problematic passengers who refused to pay. Moreover, some men who worked on the trams did not like the idea of women working on the lines. The article below touches on some of these issues as well as referring to the frisson of accidental contact with a male passenger. Liverpool's female conductors started work, in November 1915. In June 1915 Glasgow was one of the first cities to employ female tram conductors, and the Scottish city also employed female tram drivers. A recommendation that women be trained to drive trams in Wallasey was rejected by the borough council: 'it was pointed out that steep gradients, such as that of Rowson-street, were quite enough even for men drivers'.[8]

To be responsible for even the very remotest ripple of excitement in such stirring times as these is certainly some accomplishment. And that it has taken the ladies to accomplish it is only further evidence of the change in the relation of man and woman that is being wrought by the war. There is an old saying to the effect that 'Man is an adaptable animal,' but recent events go to show that woman is equally so. The latest and perhaps best example of this … is the introduction of [sic] lady car conductor. In Birkenhead this fascinating product of the war made its debut on Monday. And, as already hinted, their appearance on the cars on the Prenton and Higher Tranmere routes, where their probationary services began, created considerable interest.

And the interest aroused by these ladies in blue – for their uniform is blue, of a serviceable but none the less artistic pattern – is a pleasurable interest …

'First rate; a lot better than some of the men we have had lately.' Such was the verdict of an inspector at Woodside, who was interviewed yesterday by an 'Advertiser' representative as to the result of the first-day's work of the lady conductors. 'They have thrown themselves into the work heart and soul,' he continued; 'and they are so keen they want to get on the busy routes right away; they are not at all anxious to have the easy trips.' The driver of one of the cars on which the new conductors are being tried also testified to the efficacy of his lady assistant. 'I hardly noticed any difference,' he remarked; 'she might have been born on a car.'

One of the ladies, a little dark-haired, bright-eyed girl, who looked ready for anyone from a dock-labourer to a member of parliament, expressed herself delighted with her new job, and did not appear at all disillusioned after the first day. On the contrary she said she found the work very much more interesting than she expected. 'Of course,' she said, 'keeping our feet has been the chief trouble so far; but we shall be all right when we get our car-legs. I slipped on more than one gentleman's knee yesterday,' she added with a smile: 'And one man had his wife with him!'

Referring to the passengers, she said, 'I got on splendidly with them all, especially the men. Some of the women had their noses in the air a bit; but I suppose that was just a little jealousy because we have been in the limelight. One man tried to be funny, but I soon settled him. He said he wasn't going to pay his fare to me; so I just stopped the car and said: "Now you have either got to pay your fare or get off this car, which are you going to do?" It made him look a bit small in front of the people. Of course I had a conductor with me, but I didn't need his help.' The newcomers are being paid the same wages as their male colleagues, and whilst their engagement is only temporary, Mr Cyril Clarke, the tramways manager, entertains no doubt of their capacity or their ability to learn the intricacies of the business very rapidly.[9]

Despite being arduous, working in a rural setting had more in common with traditional female roles than factory work. Helping to feed the

Getting her 'car-legs': A female tram conductor in Birkenhead. (Author's collection)

nation was far more feminine than constructing weapons. Yet not all female factory workers constructed artillery shells. By March 1918, 8,403 women were employed by the Royal Flying Corps, of which 263 were fitters, 899 sailmakers and 153 riggers.[10] By the time this advert was placed, the nature of work at shell factories would have been well-known. The reference to the relatively less arduous nature of fuselage work suggests that some women may have been put off by work in shell factories. Health inspectors were only sent to assess the medical provision at munitions factories from May 1917.

As will be seen by the Liverpool Education Committee's advertisement that appears in this issue, the Ministry of Munitions has selected Liverpool as a centre for training women for aeroplane fuselage work, and, as the matter is one of national urgency, no time is being lost in making all the necessary arrangements locally for an early commencement, under the auspices of the Technical Education Sub-Committee, of the classes at the Central Technical School, Byrom-street. On behalf of the Local Training Committee, therefore, Mr J. G. Legge, the Director of Education, is inviting applications from women possessing a good standard of education who would be willing to undergo this special training.

The work is of the nature of light metal plate work, involving the accurate use of hand tools and measuring instruments, and, though it will make a fair demand upon the physique it will not necessitate the heavy lifting operations characteristic of the work in shell factories. The trainees will be occupied in their duties for about eight hours a day during the period of a month or thereabouts, and they will be subject to conditions approximating to those of an aeroplane factory. The training is free, but it should be noted that the trainees are required to give an undertaking to enter a munitions factory at the end of the course. The Ministry of Munitions has sanctioned the payment of a maintenance allowance of 12s per week to the women who satisfy the conditions of training.

On the conclusion of the course of training arrangements will be made by the training departments of the Ministry of Munitions to allocate the trainees to aeroplane factories in different parts of the country, where they will receive the ordinary wages payable for the class of work for which they may be engaged. This may be expected to be about 22s 6d a week at the beginning, and as the women increase in skilfulness considerably higher remuneration will be obtainable.

It is anticipated that there will be no difficulty in obtaining a good number of intelligent women from whom the first class will be selected. The fact that the work is interesting and novel will be sufficient to attract the type of women whose patriotism includes a willingness to submit to a term of instruction that she may in a better and fuller measure give her abilities and expend her energies in the service of her country.[11]

There was much discussion about alcohol during the First World War and restrictions were enforced to ensure that strong drink would not harm the war effort. Even so, people still drank. Female drinkers faced more criticism than their male counterparts. Among other things, commentators stressed that they were responsible for the next, post-war generation. This argument touched on ideas of the health of the nation rather than the more traditional moral condemnation of the Victorian era.[12] The visibility of women drinking in public houses disconcerted many observers. As this report shows, however, the police were aware that public drinking did not necessarily cause more disorder than drinking in private. In this instance the police would have gained the support of the Women's Freedom League (WFL), a breakaway movement from the WSPU. As well as campaigning for the vote, the WFL argued that women should be allowed to serve and be served in public houses.

Both encouraging and unsavoury features were presented in statements made at the Annual Licensing Meeting held in Bootle Court House on Wednesday. The licensed houses had been well conducted during the past year but there was a regrettable increase in drinking among women ...

The Chief Constable (Mr J. Stewart) in his report respecting the working of the Licensing Laws for the year 1916, said the Licensed premises in the borough number 58 and as the estimated population is about 75,000 there is one license to every 1,293 inhabitants ...

For drunkenness and for disorderly conduct whilst drunk, proceedings were taken in 154 cases. This is a decrease of 148 when compared with the figures of 1915. Of those convicted 50 were described as non-resident and 91 residing in the borough. For drunkenness occurring between 12 noon and mid-night on Sundays 11 males and 2 females were convicted, an increase of 2 when compared with last year's figures. For being drunk in charge of a child under seven years of age there was only one conviction as against seven last year. Two males were convicted of being drunk and refusing to quit licensed premises.

The decrease in the number of arrests for drunkenness is very substantial and on the whole very satisfactory, but in considering the value to be placed on these figures it must be borne in mind that a police force reduced to half its normal strength (on account of the war) cannot hope to deal with this matter as effectively as in times of peace.

The number of women drinking in public houses is largely in excess of last year's figures, and the practice is not confined to any particular part of the town. In every public-house in the borough, with five exceptions, more women were found drinking. It is difficult to understand why women in such numbers should prefer the public-house when they could drink as they wanted at home. Whatever the reason may be, there is no doubt that the practice is rapidly growing, as will be seen from the following table.

I will take only a few houses where the aggregate number of women found drinking exceeded 1,000 during the year: A.H., 1914: 608, 1915: 957, 1916: 1,467; F.A.H., 153, 584, 1,009; L. M., 916, 2,136, 4,863; M. A. H., 571, 1231, 2,830; Q.A.H., 705, 1,154, 1,390; S. G. H., 604, 1038, 1399; S. W. H., 748, 978, 1,429; W. H., 113, 712, 1,093; totals: 1914 4,418, 1915, 8,790, 1916, 14,978.

In the early part of the year the magistrates had quite a number of cases of 'women's squabbles' to deal with, and the evidence in most of the cases pointed to 'home drinking' as the cause of the trouble. Although more women are drinking than formerly, there are not many drinking to excess. The percentage of convictions of women is less than it was ten years ago, and complaints of neglect of children are very few. From time to time your Bench has asked licensees to discourage drinking amongst women on licensed premises, but so long as it is not illegal to so, no doubt the practice will continue and however desirable it may be to bring about an alteration I am convinced that nothing short of legislation to that end will be effective.[13]

Not all men were overly concerned about women drinking alcohol. Naturally, with so many men heading to the front, pub owners and members of the brewing trade like Alderman Salvidge were concerned about their trade. Salvidge feared that the recent Intoxicating Liquor (Temporary Restrictions) Act, which allowed military authorities to request that opening hours be limited in areas of military significance, would be the thin end of a wedge that would cripple the brewing industry. Like the Head Constable of Bootle in 1917, Liverpool's Head Constable was not unduly concerned with the rates of conviction for drunkenness in 1914. For others, however, the provision of relief for women whose husbands had joined the army or navy had led to a social problem that needed to be remedied by changing opening hours. There was also the associated risk of women tempting military men to drink and this was something of particular concern in port and garrison towns.

The questions of curtailing the hours of the public-houses of the city and of alleged excessive drinking among the wives of soldiers serving with the colours were again raised at a meeting of the Liverpool City Justices, at the Town Hall, yesterday. The Lord Mayor presided. No resolutions were passed in regard to either subject.

Mr S. Skelton asked if anything could be done by way of restricting the hours of the public-houses during the present crisis. He was aware that the matter rested for the moment largely with the Head Constable, but he wished to know if the Licensing Committee saw any prospect of a change. He thought it was a mistake to leave the matter in the hands of one man, and that would probably be remedied when Parliament assembled again.

Sir Thomas Hughes, chairman of the Licensing Committee, said that the committee had had two meetings and had consulted the Head Constable. Practically, the committee had no power at all except on the recommendation of the Head Constable, and on both occasions Mr Caldwell had said that drunkenness was normal – indeed, that the number of cases twelve months ago was very much greater than they were to-day – and that therefore he could make no recommendation about altering the hours of opening and closing ...

Alderman Salvidge said that the licensed trade had expressed its willingness to the Head Constable and the military commander to carry out during the crisis the slightest wish of the military authorities. The recent Act was passed not to advance temperance legislation but to meet the military situation, and the crisis should not be used to ventilate or advance any particular view on the licensing question ...

Sir Thomas Hughes: Will Mr Salvidge answer this important question? What are you prepared to do in regard to serving women?

Alderman Salvidge said it was not fair to ask him such a question. If the magistrates thought there was undue drinking among women let them voluntarily bring pressure to bear on the trade ...

Now that two of the Dale-street courts are being occupied largely with the hearing of cases, often of wounding, which have arisen out of the congregation of drinking parties of women held in private houses, public opinion seems to be ripening in favour of drastic remedies for this social evil (writes a correspondent). Even under the existing law much more might be done to punish the women who aid and abet the crimes following from the demoralisation which ensues when women join in debauchery. ... It would be a gross libel on most of the wives of soldiers and sailors to say that they spend their separation allowances in drunken orgies, but there is a small percentage of cases where the allowances do go to fill the gallon beer jugs, and in such payment in coin ought not to be continued. In certain districts not far from the city the supply of beer to women has had to be prohibited because of the temptation offered by females of low degree to small coteries of reservists or recruits excluded from the canteens.[14]

Margaret Beavan was educated at Liverpool High School and decided to end her degree studies at Royal Holloway College so she could dedicate her energies to voluntary work. Beavan set up convalescent homes for children and arranged for children from slums to have breaks in the countryside. Later, she established the Royal Liverpool Babies Hospital and became lord mayor in 1926. As a Conservative, Beavan thought that assistance for the needy was something that should be provided by voluntary means rather than the state. Yet she was no moralist. Mothers in need were mothers, whether they were married or not. Beavan was criticised for visiting Italy while she was mayor. One of her detractors, the Labour Councillor Margaret Simey, called her 'Maggie Mussolini'.[15]

In the last year of the war Miss Beavan introduced an unusual little experiment with regard to unmarried mothers and their babies. The scheme arose from an incident at hospital which she herself related as follows:

'A discerning physician in the out-patient department of the Children's Infirmary, who had been carefully examining a wasted, wailing infant, turned to the I.C.A. (Invalid Children's Aid) representative who was awaiting instructions and laconically ejaculated "Mothering: provide that!" and he further added, "Why not spend the money you would spend on hospital treatment in providing the mother's care?" It transpired that the mother was unmarried and had to work to support herself and her infant, who was left to the ignorant care of a neighbour, with the result that many pounds had to be expended to bring that infant back to life.'

Miss Beavan had been very much impressed by this incident and, accepting the challenge, she launched the scheme whereby allowances were made by the Association to twenty unmarried mothers or young widows to enable them to stay at home and nurse their babies. The scheme was encouraged by the Medical Officer of Health and the municipality, though not able to undertake a scheme of this kind for itself, nevertheless made a grant of 50 per cent towards the cost.

Though only a small scheme, it was a very successful one, since in order to qualify for the grant the young mothers were obliged to attend the clinic and give an account of their own diet and child's progress. Sometimes the cases were disappointing, for a careless or 'hardened' young woman occasionally resisted all efforts to make her care for a child which she obviously did not want; but in the majority of cases the result was to bring about an increase of a sense of responsibility on the mother's part, and the supervision did her a great deal of good. It is interesting to note that this scheme was not made a moral issue in any way – except in so far as the teaching of responsibility was a moral influence. The Association was concerned only with the health of mother and child. Sympathy was given, and advice if the mother asked for it; often she needed help in the vexed question of affiliation orders or other problems of a social nature in which the Association could be of real use, and this was gladly given; but allusion to the 'sins' of the young mother were refreshingly absent and this fact proves the experiment to be a pioneer one, both in its practice and in its attitude to the girls who benefitted.[16]

With the outbreak of war, landladies found themselves on the front line of the home front. If they had lodgers from abroad, they may be inadvertently sheltering spies. The transient lodger was more of a threat to the nation than the respectable German shop owner. Lodgers may have been less visible than German businesses, but they were able to move from town to town and conceal their activities. This report of a court case shows how the war entered people's homes and businesses. Many women subsidised their income by renting rooms, and as long as the rent was paid and the tenant behaved they paid little attention to their lodgers' nationality. Given the reputation of landladies for being stern and territorial, it is no surprise that this policeman who did not display due deference was given a frosty reception.[17]

Two Runcorn landladies appeared before Bench at Monday's Runcorn Sessions summoned for sins of omission in connection with the orders relating to aliens residing in their houses. The first defendant was Mrs Alice Smidie, of Peel street, against whom were two summonses, the first under the September Order with failing to furnish particulars of aliens staying in her house, and the second, under the special order issued in prohibited areas, charging her with having failed to ascertain the nationality and other particulars of aliens staying in her house and failing to keep a register in which such particulars should be entered.

Margaret Beavan – philanthropist and Liverpool's first female Lord Mayor. (Author's collection)

With respect to the second summons, Superintendent Owen said that under the Aliens Restriction Act, 1915, after the 25th April, it was the duty of every lodging-house keeper to ascertain and enter in a register the nationality and other particulars of all aliens in the house over fourteen. After the issue of the order Detective Sergeant Davies was sent round to every lodging-house keeper – a term which included managers of hotels and all who let lodgings – and handed to each two forms, one which every lodger had to fill up and the other a form of register for aliens. The defendant had failed to fill up these forms or to keep a register according to the regulations. The sergeant explained to each exactly what had to be done.

Detective Sergeant Davies said that on April 27th he served copies of the two forms upon the defendant. He fully explained what had to be done and told her what the penalty would be. He called again on June 5th and examined a form which had been filled up by Mr and Mrs Stein, the former being described as an American and the latter as English. He asked the defendant if she had kept a register and she produced 'form A.R.S.,' which had been supplied for her guidance. She said that when she asked Mr Stein to fill it up he said he was 'not an alien, but an American.' She also said she had not reported it to the police and didn't seem to understand. Mr and Mrs Stein had not registered in the aliens register.

Defendant: I didn't understand.

The Clerk: But the sergeant explained to you.

Defendant: He came in rather a rough way, I asked him to call again when the gentleman came in, but he said he had no time.

Sergeant Davies: I pointed it out to her daughter aged seventeen, but she seemed to pooh-pooh the thing entirely.

The Clerk: The police could not have rendered any more assistance. They went round and explained personally.

The Chairman (Mr A. Norman) said the defendant ought to have acquainted herself with all the details of these Acts which would have to be strictly carried out. That was the first case the Bench had had before them, and he hoped it would be a warning to the defendant and everyone else who was interested. A fine of 10s in each case would be imposed.

Superintendent Owen said that summonses had been issued against Mr and Mrs Stein for failing to register, but had not been served.

The second defendant was Mrs Cohen of Waterloo road, represented by Mr H. N. Linaker. She pleaded guilty to failing to keep a register.[18]

This editorial has a jocular tone but it deals with a serious topic: national registration. The need to identify and channel national resources led to the National Registration Act of July 1915. All men and women between the ages of fifteen and sixty-five were to provide information about their work, home and skills. Men filled in a blue form, while women completed a white form. All those eligible also had to inform the authorities when they moved. The deadline for submission was midnight Sunday 15 August, and the enumerator would call to collect the forms between 16 and 21 August. At the end of the process, the certificate that was given to the individual was effectively an identity 'card'. The editorial also indicates the 'typical' woman's role on a Sunday. The contrast between the Sunday dinner and the form captures the collision between the domestic life and a national crisis.

There is likely to be considerable interference with Sunday's cooking arrangements, for that Registration form has to be filled up, and a great number of Liverpool housewives have to decide whether they are under or over sixty-five years of age. Ladies are often accused of taking minimum views as to their ages, but on this occasion there is a strong temptation to stretch a point in the other direction, and so escape liability to be called out on war-work. It is a case requiring considerable deliberation on the part of house-wives, and while the deliberation is proceeding the cooking will probably be forgotten, and many a husband may arrive home hungry only to discover that the Sunday joint has been cremated and the vegetables incinerated. Thus Registration is certainly the cause of much perturbation all over the country, and all the men and most of the women believe there is 'something behind it.' And no doubt there is, but it isn't Conscription, which would require a new Act of Parliament, which might be very difficult to pass considering the working classes of

England are almost to a man opposed to it as unnecessary and uncalled for. So let us fill up our Registration forms without fear and trembling, and regard the process as just one more precaution in the very unlikely event of things coming to the worst. Housewives would be well-advised if they postponed the ordeal of filling up their papers until the afternoon, so as not to disturb the family temper by spoiling the Sunday dinner.[19]

How did mothers, wives and children cope while their sons, husbands and fathers were away? Allowances provided material assistance while family and neighbours provided emotional support. Not knowing about their son's whereabouts or condition would place great strain on mothers and other relatives. What is often overlooked, however, is that the men at war were also upset when they did not hear news from home. An examination of letters from the front can tell us something about the relationship between mothers and sons, husbands and wives and fathers and children. In the following examples, mothers refer to the end of the war and remind readers that they are thinking of those at the front. Being a mother took on an added significance during the war. Their sons may sacrifice their lives, but mothers were asked to sacrifice the sons.

The Mothers' Page

We are glad to pass on the messages sent by several mothers of the 'Boys'. The mothers are feeling the strain of war as much as anyone. All honour to British motherhood which has given ungrudgingly of its very best!

Mrs North writes 'Dear Mr Editor – It is with pleasure that I accept your kind invitation to write a letter in the Mothers' Page of Y.C. In the first place I appreciate your efforts in publishing each month news from all the boys connected with Crescent who so nobly responded to the call – 'Your King and Country need you!' Their letters are read eagerly by one and all, and one cannot fail to notice how cheerfully they write, which is a source of comfort to us. We, the mothers of the Boys must keep a good heart and hope and pray for a safe return to civil life for them all.' (80 Aubrey St Walton)

Mrs Horrocks – 'Dear Crescent Boys – I am glad to know many of you and I read YC eagerly for news of you all. I wish with all my heart that this cruel war was over and that I could see you all, along with my own three lads in dear old Everton again.' (2 College St)

Mrs Mackie 'Dear Crescent Boys – I gladly avail myself of this privilege to extend my greetings to all of you serving your King and Country. I can assure you everybody at Crescent is looking forward to the day when peace will be declared and the Boys be amongst them again. Your reception will be a great one, I assure you.' (29 Gilroy Rd)

Mrs D. Mair – 'Dear Crescent Boys – I thought I would send you a few lines to let you know how 'Young Crescent' is appreciated in India. I have been sending a copy each month to a soldier stationed in Burmah. This is what he says in reply for the Jan no. 'I had quite a lot of after me for the Y. C., and now one of the secretaries of the Y.M.C.A. has got it to hand round their members as they like it too. It tells them how the Boys go on at the Front.' …

Mrs Singleton – 'Dear Boys – It gives me the greatest pleasure to write you a line through this wonderful volume. You cannot tell how I look forward to the coming of the magazine, and when I have read it, I am eagerly waiting for the next. We receive news not only of our own lads, but others as well, and although I do not know you all, your letters are always welcome. I wish you all God speed and a safe return.'

Mrs Evans – 'Dear Boys – I am glad to take this opportunity of thanking you all for your very kind expressions of sympathy, and thoughtful letters received from you in connection with the passing away of my boy and your companion. Although I do not know many of you personally, I know you well by name, and hope you are all making the best of your circumstances, and living the best life.'

FATHERS – It is your turn to fill this page next month![20]

One of the few Merseyside women to write up her memories of the war years was Agnes Cowper. Although she was seventy-five when she published her memoirs, Cowper vividly recalls the news that her brother had survived the sinking of the *Lusitania*. Her description of the scene at Woodside Station provides a rare account of the raw and public sorrow felt by those who discovered that their loved-ones would not return. A member of the Salvation Army was at hand to comfort the bereaved. Train stations are places where people depart and return. During the war, return was in no way guaranteed.

We did not retire, for sleep would have been impossible. We were doing our best to convince each other that the morrow would bring good news when, at one a.m., came a ring at the bell, and mother cried, 'Thank God, he is safe.' And sure enough, there in the doorway stood a telegraph messenger holding the familiar orange-coloured envelope which held the message, 'Saved. Ernest.' A short time ago I had the occasion to search among my mother's papers and found this telegraph put carefully away. It was evidently one of her family treasures.

On the following morning I arrived at the Dingle Station of the Overhead Railway, where it came as a great surprise to me to be confronted with the large newspaper placard of a well-known pictorial daily bearing a picture of my brother Ernest holding a small child whom, as I later learned from the paper, he had been instrumental in saving from the wreck. Later in the day another telegram arrived, saying, 'Will arrive Sunday afternoon five-fifteen Woodside Station.'

Early as I was, others were earlier, including some who, with little children, had kept an all-night vigil on one of our Liverpool stations where two trains had arrived, one in the early hours of the morning and one at mid-day. Although each had brought a little company of survivors, no familiar face had gladdened the hearts of these weary watchers. Though no message of promise had reached them they had heard that the last of the saved would arrive at Woodside Station at five-fifteen, and hope, sometimes so cruel, bade them forget their fatigue and the weary watches of the night, and led them, dragging and carrying little children, to resume their watch at Woodside ...

At last the train was signalled; a silence, weird and awesome, fell upon us broken only by the voice of a little child calling 'Want to go home mummy, want to go home.' I saw the Salvationist relieve the woman of her infant; and then the train came steaming in. Oh! The mingled joy and agony of the next few seconds as carriage doors were flung open giving back, as from the dead, a few, but alas, for that tragic group, not one. Then a woman's voice was heard calling, 'Has no one seen my Jim?' The returned survivors were greeted in silence by her friends who, in the face of so much stark sorrow, seemed to realise that audible expressions of their own great joy would be hardly less than an outrage. My brother was caught and held by women who eagerly accosted him with questions as 'Mister, did you see a big tall man anywhere; my husband?'[21]

With the advent of conscription at the start of 1916, even more attention turned to those who were left behind. A man who provided for a family or assisted a family member may have refrained from joining the army for fear of leaving their relatives in poverty. For some the support was not merely financial, emotional needs were also taken into consideration. The following letter refers to the sensitive issue of widows' sons being sent to the front by the tribunals that had been set up to select men for the military. Its author, H. Bradshaw, is very critical of how the tribunal system had treated the sons.

Dear Sir, Will you permit me through the medium of your paper, to call attention to the kindlier atmosphere of the local Tribunal as far as widows' sons are concerned?

In the earlier stages the military machine ruthlessly devoured all who came across its path, and consequently it is not surprising to find that cases of gross injustice have been recorded. Widows' sons were given a scant month, or even less, to set their houses in order, and this despite the Government promise that only in the case of direst necessity would they be called upon. This week, however, many widows' sons have been granted exemption until September, showing that the Tribunal has at last realised how barbarous its former decisions have been.

What I wish to point out is this, that where an appeal has been heard and exemption granted the appellant is entitled to appeal again before his period of exemption has expired. Now, judging by the Tribunal records, there must have been a number of local widows' sons who have been harshly treated, and it is in the hope of reaching these men that I am asking for space in your paper.

Will all widows' sons who have appealed, and who have a cause for complaint with the Tribunal's decision, take steps to lodge a further appeal, providing they are not too late, as I am sure they will receive more consideration now, and they will be helping, incidentally, to lessen the adverse criticism levelled at the Tribunals by righteously indignant individuals?

Yours sincerely,

H. Bradshaw,

18 Liversidge Road, Birkenhead.[22]

As the war went on, attention turned to the welfare of the next generation. A national 'Baby Week' was inaugurated in July 1917. While some have seen this as an attempt to encourage women to 'produce more future soldiers', there was also a desire to improve the conditions of working-class households and reduce infant and maternal mortality.[23] This account of the 'invasion' of the Town Hall by mothers and babies was a public demonstration of interest in the lives of working-class mothers by the local government and charitable bodies. In doing so they were also showing an interest in the future of the city. During the week, films and demonstrations were put on to educate mothers about infant health care. Different places marked the week in their own way, Bootle and Southport provided more energetic activities than Liverpool. Bootle had a fifteen-foot baby race for babies less than fifteen months of age and there was a pram parade in Southport.[24]

The baby battalion attacked the civic headquarters of Liverpool to-day. They forced an entry and consolidated their position at the tea table. The captured staff headed by the Lady Mayoress, surrendered with a smile, and fraternised freely with their captors.

Those who witnessed the assault were delighted with the condition of the troops. Their uniform was of the whitest, their faces shone with health, and their battle cry, given with no uncertain voice, came as from people who know what they wanted and were determined to have it. Each warrior had his or her mother in attendance.

This reception of mothers and babes at the Town Hall was a great success, and the interest which the Lady Mayoress showed in the 'tots' pleased the mothers greatly. There was a truly wonderful assortment. There were babies dark and babies fair, small babies and big babies, babies that looked upon the proceedings with a happy smile, and babies who would not be comforted ...

Altogether some 600 babies and their mothers were present.

This was only one item in the second day's programme for 'baby week.' The Liverpool babies had been receiving mayoral appreciation for many hours previously. The little ones in the Abercromby House Day Nursery had been visited by the Lady Mayoress and the baronet doctor (Sir Francis Champneys), and visit was paid to the two other day nurseries – 19, Beaumont-street, and 87, South Hill-street.

The city has to-day increased its day nurseries by four. One has been opened at Elms House, 407, Edge-lane; another at 264, Westminster-road, another at 332, Netherfield-road, and another at 19, Great George-square.

Another feature of the day has been an exhibition by the Liverpool Ladies' Sanitary Association, showing how to make babies' food and clothes. Then there have been consultations, during which doctors ran over the little ones with a foot measure and treated their chests as though practicing on the keyboard of a typewriter.

The infants were put on scales and weighed – at least those who did not turn out to be truculent resisters, and there were certainly a few who showed signs of pugilistic intentions.

If the verdict of the doctors all over the country on the nation's babies is similar to the one arrived at over the Liverpool babies, the rising generation is a 'promising crop.'[25]

In 1976, Peter Liddle interviewed Margaret Rankine. She was born in Flintshire in 1894 and moved with her family to Merseyside, where her father was a miller. Margaret had four brothers: two were in the navy at the outbreak of the war, another lived in

Canada and the youngest was at home. Seeing as she was the only daughter, it is no surprise that her father was reluctant for her to take on an onerous occupation. Liddle interviewed Rankine after receiving a letter describing her wartime experiences. The two accounts contain some significant differences – the interview includes elements that she omitted in her memoirs.

Peter Liddle (PL): How soon was it that you felt some call to do your own bit for the war effort?

Margaret Rankine (MR): Well, the boys had all gone you see and I was alone. I saw a friend of my father's and I said, I want to be a nurse. Will you introduce me to a hospital because I didn't know anything about hospitals and I had talked to my father before that I wanted to be a nurse. He said, no. I won't allow you, it is too hard a life. However, I went to this friend of my father's and he said, yes, I will give you a letter to the Matron of the Children's Hospital in Liverpool.

[The matron advised Margaret to get her general training then come back to work with children and she undertook her general training at Mill Road Hospital, Liverpool.]

PL: What was your motivation initially to nurse wounded soldiers?

MR: No. I always wanted to be a nurse. All my dolls were always sick. They were always bandaged and everybody had to be quiet and this sort of thing. It was just instinctive that I loved sick people ...

[Rankine then recalls her first day on the ward.]

MR: I put my cap on back to front which sister put all the way round properly and I went into the kitchen and the nurse disappeared. There was a maid washing up and I said, what do I do. She said, go to the top and scrub macintoshes. I said, where is the top. Well, she said, the top of the ward you fool. Thank you. So, I walked up the ward and there were forty men and I felt myself getting hotter and hotter. My collar getting tighter. I had seen my brothers in bed but I had never seen forty men. Some with their arms stuck up here and some with their legs stuck up here and I thought will I ever get to the top of this ward. It is so long. However, a man said to me, nurse, can I have a bottle. I said certainly. So I went into the bathroom and I took a hot water bottle down and filled it. Nice and hot. I let the water run and I wiped it and I put a cover on it and I went in and stood and he just disappeared down the bed with laughter and all round the ward.

So with that the nurse came to me and took me by the shoulder and she said, you fool. She said, come and I will show you what a bottle is ...

PL: Now in what state in regard to earlier treatment of wounds or being washed down were these men coming in off the convoys?

MR: Straight from France. Straight out of the trenches. They had still got their dirty clothes on with the mud on them and as the orderlies and we took their boots off their foot came with it. They were gangrenous. They had been lying in France for a week, most of them. They didn't remember but the orderlies said that they had gone out to find if there were any living on the field after the Battle of the Somme and they had found them. Some were still breathing and they had been there a solid week. They were in a dreadful state.[26]

The scale of medical services mobilised on the home front during the First World War is revealed in this extract about a Voluntary Aid Detachment (VAD) hospital in Southport. According to Thekla Bowser, who was an Honorary Sister of the Order of St John, the

Shy but determined: Margret Rankine in the middle row. (Courtesy of Brotherton Library, University of Leeds WW1/WO/098)

VAD brought together volunteers from a variety of backgrounds. They wore the same uniform and experienced similar conditions. Although Bowser does not make much of the division between qualified nurses and volunteers, the difference between the two groups would also have given the volunteers a clear identity. Some volunteers were nicknamed 'Very Able Dusters'.[27] Despite often being of a higher social class than the nurses they worked with, VAD workers had to work hard to demonstrate their worth.

In Lancashire there is the largest VAD hospital in the United Kingdom, and it is run by St. John Detachments. It is situated in The Grange and Woodlands, Southport, and has 500 beds. In December 1915, the Director-General of Medical Services visited the hospital and said that it must become a Primary one instead of an Auxiliary. When it was found that its accommodation must be increased by having open-air huts set up, the work was effected in seven weeks at The Grange, the ground which had been a kitchen garden being quickly converted into the site of a very up-to-date hospital.

Here we see another branch of VAD work, which again is typical of what is going on in every district. VAD pharmacists in this hospital have control of an enormous store of dressings and drugs. Three-quarters of a ton of cotton wool, and 10,000 yards of gauze, bought in the cheapest competitive market, is an incident in their work ... VAD members are in the dispensary during the day, but do no technical work, of course.

The kitchen VAD members here have no sinecure. For instance, the daily peeling and slicing of 186 lb of potatoes, the cleaning of 200 knives, forks, and spoons, the scouring of sinks and boilers, is a magnificent piece of voluntary work of which Southport may be justly proud.

Blanket Day

This was a bright idea, a reception being held in Hesketh Park, admission being by blanket, which raised a thousand of these necessary articles.

Linen Department

The lady quartermasters have organised this department, an enormous amount of repairing and stitching having been done there; 4,479 yards of material have been cut out in the hospital itself and made up by voluntary workers. On an average over 11,000 articles are sent daily to the laundry, so that some idea of the amount of work entailed can be gained. Over 1,500 things pass through the hands of the linen-room staff every day at the Grange alone![28]

Both of the following extracts are about Liverpool women who gained some degree of celebrity during the war. Nora Hackett worked with the French Red Cross and reported her experiences to the *Liverpool Courier* in 1915. Her comments about the bureaucracy that accompanied getting a passport indicate her eagerness to get to the front. Later, her assessment of the French Red Cross suggests that she may have regretted volunteering to work with the organisation. Nonetheless, others were excited by the prospect of working on hospital trains because it brought them closer to the front line.[29] Theresa Edgar, of Oriel Road, Aintree, was a stewardess and the only female on the Cunard ocean liner *Ausonia* that left Liverpool for New York in May 1918. The ship was followed by U-boats but the accompanying destroyers dropped depth charges and departed after assuming that the submarines had given up the chase. However, on 30 May 1918 about 620 miles off Fastnet, the ship, which had played a part in the evacuation from Gallipoli in January 1916, was attacked and sunk with the loss of forty-four crew members. Edgar was interviewed after the war and her account of the sinking contains plenty of drama and humour.

It was no easy matter getting over to France. In spite of the fact that I had my Paris papers of residence, I had to go through the same forms as all other intending travellers. This means applying at the Foreign Office for a passport application form, which has to be filled and the most searching questions answered; a J.P., magistrate, or doctor of medicine, law or religion, must stand as reference; and, when all this has been done some days of patient waiting must be endured. Then another trip to the Foreign Office, another form; and, finally the passport from Sir Edward Grey, Baronet of the United Kingdom, and so on, requesting all whom it may concern to allow free passage, etc., etc., is obtained. The photograph of the intending traveller has to be fixed on the passport, and then the French Consul stamps it.

Finally all was settled, and with big red crosses stuck all over the boxes which contained several thousands of cigarettes, provided for the soldiers by Miss D. Cross of Castle-street, the secretary of the 'Have One of Mine from Liverpool' society, I started off. According to instructions, all travellers had to present themselves at least an hour before the timed departure of the train so that their luggage and they themselves could be thoroughly searched. Victoria platform was thronged by officers and men returning after the 'seventy-two hours' leave. All the women except eight who travelled over looked anxious, and the men had a quietly alert air of readiness. In the dining car, at my table, there was a R.A.M.C. [Royal Army Medical Corps] man and two lieutenants of cavalry. 'When I ordered my tub this morning,' one of them said to his friend 'I told my man, "This will probably be the last I shall have for many days," and he asked in great astonishment, "Aren't there any baths in Berlin, sir?"'

Then came the crossing, about as bad as it could be; but I and my luggage landed safely at —, well, somewhere in France. The following day I visited some of the hospitals, distributing cigarettes, handkerchiefs, and real English wax matches, not the sulphurous 'portable 'ells' as one indignant Tommy called the French lights! From this place I succeeded in getting on to =, but perhaps I had better not name the place. It was swarming with English to such an extent that had Mary Tudor had a vision of it as it is to-day, she would certainly have cancelled the post-mortem inscription on her heart! I heard that the list of victims of an aerial raid was daily increasing, but I found the townspeople calm and absolutely convinced of ultimate victory.

In both towns the British Red Cross hospitals were excellent, and the wet roads were churned by the constantly passing neat grey motor ambulances which tore along the coast road with their burdens of maimed humanity. I – who had been working with the *Croix Rouge* on the cattle trains in Valois, where the French wounded spent days in jolting darkness; hungry, thirsty, and cold – could not restrain a feeling of envy when I saw the expeditiousness, cleanliness, and order of the British medical arrangements.[30]

You might have thought Theresa Edgar would never again be found on an ocean ship. If you had gone through her ordeal you probably would feel that you had a right to a prejudice. And yet she has just 'gone back.' Perhaps the lure of the sea was too strong for any counter prejudice. And besides, there are no more submarines ...

[O]f all the thrilling encounters with submarines which the war produced, that told by a young English woman who spent eight days in a lifeboat until finally picked up by a British destroyer, is in some ways the most thrilling.

One can understand how a seafaring man would have the pride to resent being driven from the sea by a little experience with a submarine which cast him afloat on the broad blue ocean.

But this is the story of a little woman, who, lover of the sea, and fearless to the last degree, has, after those terrible days last year in an open boat, courageously put to sea again as stewardess of the big Cunard Liner, the *Orduna*, which plied continually between American and British ports, and transported thousands of American soldiers and war workers during the entire war period ...

Mrs Edgar, the young widow of a seafaring man, has a considerable war record herself, for aside from her terrible experience after being torpedoed, she has successfully crisscrossed the Atlantic danger zone sixty times ...

'Late Thursday afternoon, being very tired and having nothing to do, I lay down in my cabin and was soon fast asleep. A terrible explosion awakened me a little while later. It was about 5 o'clock. Thinking the danger had passed when I lay down, I took off my blue dress and slipped on my kimono. I had my shoes on.

'Merely curious, I walked out into the alleyway, when the chief steward came rushing down the stairs. "For God's sake," he called to me, "get on your lifebelt! The boat is sinking!"

'I hurried on deck and saw that the stern was dipping down into the sea ...

'I had just bought a new spring hat in London,' she said. 'It was a pretty shade of pink. I liked it better than any hat I had ever had. I rushed back and got that hat. That is the only thing I saved ...

'There were seven lifeboats in all. The submarine when it saw our men could not operate our ship's guns, came to the surface, and running in between us, fired about forty rounds into the *Ausonia*. The ship seemed fairly to leap out of the sea, stood for a fleeting minute on her nose, as it were, and dropped into the water.

'With the Germans standing at their guns, the captain of the submarine whipped out a revolver, and pointing it at the men in the different lifeboats ordered them to come alongside ...

'When he spied my pink hat, he seemed surprised, and remarked in perfect English to his comrades, "Why, there's a lady in this boat!"'[31]

While studying for a degree at Liverpool University, Gladys Dalby New tried a variety of jobs. Even though we know that the war altered opportunities for men and women, we rarely get an insight into why particular decisions were made. This account does not conform to the popular image of women taking up opportunities to assist the war effort. Instead of serving as a nurse or other role, New followed the advice of her family and continued her studies. Her father was a transport manger at Port Sunlight and clearly

Theresa Edgar, the hat-loving stewardess. (Author's collection)

had ambitions for his children. The following is a summary of her activities during the war.

Left school just before war broke out in 1914. The war was a great shock to everyone. She had three sisters and one brother and they attended lectures on First Aid. The older girls had hospital experience but she was considered too young and was instead put with a district nurse which involved visits to private houses in terrible slum conditions in Liverpool. She found the work very interesting in spite of the squalor.

In October 1914 she went to study at Liverpool University reading five subjects, Geography being her main interest. She got her degree in 1917. She remarks on the shortage of men at university; owing to the war, young men reading medicine were the only ones in evidence.

In 1915 she and one of her sisters went each Sunday to a Liverpool military hospital to do voluntary work such as cleaning brasses and scrubbing floors. At the age of seventeen she had no particular boyfriends, not much social life. The boys she did know had joined up and were killed.

She was on the Students' Council in 1915 till 1918.

Recalls strawberry picking just outside Chester, along with a group of girls. They left, the pay being very little.

In 1918 she went to Ilchester in Somerset flax picking. They worked very hard from early morning until dusk.

During 1914 sketching overlooking Mersey she and her coach, an older lady, were arrested by two soldiers as possible spies. Her sketch was taken and shown to an officer who did not think it was good enough to be important and handed it back to her and they were free to go.

Talks about food rationing and many vegetable only pies that they ate.

She taught for a while towards the end of 1918 at the girls school Belvedere Liverpool. They had been encouraged to study rather than serve in any way during the war because there would be a severe shortage of teachers so many having been killed in the services.[32]

As this call for female police in Birkenhead shows, women were valued for their ability to supervise the young and other females.

Flax picking in Somerset during 1918. Gladys Dalby New stands fourth from left. (Courtesy of Brotherton Library, University of Leeds WW1/DF/095)

Problems like juvenile crime and prostitution could be tackled by females who patrolled the streets. Many suffragists at this time felt that they had a duty to assist vulnerable women. Yet in practice the female police were engaged in a variety of activities that ranged from the separation of overly affectionate couples in parks to patrolling and inspecting munitions factories that employed large numbers of women.[33] The second source is an interview with a former female sergeant in the Birkenhead force. Like a number of women who took up the opportunity of joining the police, Phyllis Lovell had been a schoolmistress. Her reasons for leaving the force show that she had strong opinions about the need for women to have the same responsibilities as male members of the force. In fact, she argues that in some respects women were more capable than male officers.

The advisability of having women police had been recognised in Birkenhead for a considerable time, and steps have now been taken to show that this borough is once more 'to the fore.'

The Watch Committee have given the Chief Constable (Mr Edward Parker) authority to employ women police to do certain work in the town, and the Chief Constable has the matter now under contemplation, and is prepared to receive applications from suitable women. Women with local knowledge are preferred, not more than 30 years of age, of good physique, height 5ft 5in or 5ft 6in, and they must be prepared to pass a medical examination, and also be of fair education. The Watch Committee propose to pay a commencing salary of 30s., with uniform.

With regard to the duties of such women police, we can only say at present that they would mainly be amongst the female and juvenile classes.[34]

The 'Empire' of Sunday published an interesting interview with ex-Sergt Phyllis Lovell whom it describes as the 'pioneer policewoman of Great Britain,' who recently resigned from the Birkenhead Police Force.

The trouble is that the Home Office will not permit women to be sworn in like other constables. They may be taken on as supernumeraries, but they have no powers. If they witness an illegal act they must go and fetch a real police officer.

'When permission was given to women to assist the police,' Miss Lovell explained, 'we thought we were to be sworn-in and take the duties of ordinary constables. But when I was appointed I discovered that women could not be sworn-in without a special Act of Parliament being passed.

'I suggested that the proper course would be to put an emergency measure through under the Defence of the Realm regulations, swear in women constables for the duration of the war, and at the end of the period reconsider the position and see whether the women constables had really justified themselves. The authorities have not yet seen their way to do this ...

'I am thoroughly satisfied that women constables have come to stay. They have proved their usefulness at Birkenhead, and they are recognised as efficient officers.

'We can deal with domestic cases in a way that a policeman could not, and there are frequently inquiries to be made which are impossible for a man, and there is the influence we can wield with a woman in trouble, or in connection with patrol duty, especially late at night. Then there is detective work, for which women, in my opinion, are particularly adapted.

'One of my girls was a perfect genius at disguising herself, and she met with great success in one case where male officers had failed to get the desired information.

'But, unfortunately, we were restricted in our usefulness at Birkenhead being almost entirely limited to beat and point duty.'[35]

Although more often associated with the Second World War, the Women's Land Army was founded in 1917 as result of concerns about British agricultural production. Some 45,000 had applied to serve by the end of the war, but only about half that number had the opportunity to work on farms.[36] Processions and speeches, such as the one below at Southport, featured an alternative type of femininity. Rather than caring for the conventional trappings of womanhood, Land Army girls were practical, patriotic and not afraid to work in unappealing environments. They were contrasted with what were called 'fluffy' women, each group being identified by their choice of footwear. The topic of how women should behave and dress was a recurring theme during the war.

A very successful demonstration of women land workers in support of the recruiting campaign for the Women's Land Army was held on Saturday in Southport. The recruiting campaign extends over a fortnight, and its headquarters are the Red Cross Depot, Lord street, opposite the Palladium. In the morning a band of about 70 women land workers paraded some of the principal thoroughfares. Attired in their overalls and leggings, they looked a very smart and workmanlike body as they paraded, bearing various banners which proclaimed such messages as 'Join the Land Army and Hold the Home Front,' 'Join the Land Army and go into the Country,' 'We all feel fit in the Land Army,' 'Wanted – Men in the Field, Women in the Fields,' and 'England Must be Fed.'

The morning procession was headed by the Mayoress (Mrs T. Hampson) and the Deputy-Mayor (Councillor R. Morrin). In the afternoon the principal demonstration took place. The parade was now strengthened by the presence of a number of lorries, conveying women haymakers, hay loads both trussed and untrussed, barrels of potatoes etc. Heading the procession was the band of the National Reserve, by kind permission on Mayor J. A. Pease, and following in cars were the Mayor and Mayoress (Councillor and Mrs T. Hampson), Mr Francis Ward (hon. Treasurer for the Women's Land Army in Lancashire). In addition to the Women's Land Army contingent and their officers, the procession also included a contingent of wounded soldiers from the Woodlands, a squad of Girl Guides, and the 2nd Southport Company of the Boys' Brigade, the last-mentioned under Captain T. L. Bower and Adjutant Mercier.

The Mayor presided at a meeting held at the Town Hall steps … As a result of the first day's recruiting in Southport for the Women's Land Army, a total of 50 recruits was secured. This is regarded as a very satisfactory start, and is all the more gratifying in view of the fact that some of those present in the audience addressed from the Town Hall steps at Saturday afternoon's demonstration took umbrage at some of the remarks made by one of the speakers of the Women's Land Army. This particular speaker attacked the 'fluffy' type of girl … They had got to prove to our men that they were worth fighting for. They could not do that by tripping about in silk stockings and high-heeled boots, but would do it by 'clamping' about in solid service boots, doing something worthwhile for them. As she went through the streets of Southport that day, she did not think she had ever seen so many 'fluffy' girls. They were awfully nice to look at, but she longed to jump out of the car, and get hold of them. The speaker reminded the girls in the audience that they owed their present happiness, comfort and innocence, their ability to play tennis and to do everything nearly as it was before the war, to our soldiers; and she made a strong plea for them to give something in return by joining the Land Army, and helping to secure food for them and the nation.

3

Problems on the Home Front

Liverpool had always been a departure point for transatlantic travel. The port has been likened to 'a great railway station'.[1] With the outbreak of war, however, the movement of people speeded up as anxious Americans and others from around the globe rushed back home. Unlike ports on the North Sea, Liverpool had a relatively sheltered position on the west coast. Nonetheless, the hurried departure of tourists and arrival of prisoners and wounded soldiers brought the war to Liverpool. Although some of these tourists were without their luggage, they would have carried many stories about their experiences in Europe. The *Liverpool Courier* noted that the Americans would be happy with any class of travel as long as they returned, but this appears to be contradicted in the *Liverpool Daily Post*'s report that suggests there was much demand for second class accommodation.

All this week scores of Americans have been pouring into Liverpool, many of them having had very uncomfortable experiences in getting back from the Continent. The hotels are full, and the Adelphi alone has close on 600 people anxiously waiting for steamers to take them home.

Many of them, both ladies and gentlemen, arrived without anything in the way of belongings, their trunks having gone astray on the Continent.

The intimation by the Admiralty that there are in the Atlantic 24 British cruisers in addition to French warships, protecting the trade routes, has put these stranded Americans and Canadians in good spirits, and they are now all haste to get home. They are willing to take all risks that may attend the passage across the Atlantic, and it matters not whether they go first or third class so long as they can get an early passage.

The Royal Mail Steam Packet Co. announce that their ocean yachting steamer *Arcadian* will now definitely sail from Liverpool on Monday next, the 17th inst. Direct to New York, subject only to the intervention of his Majesty's Government.[2]

The crowd of Americans in this country will be lessened before the end of the present week, as many are leaving by the White Star liners *Adriatic* and *Olympic,* the former of which leaves for New York to-day, and the latter on Saturday. Both vessels are practically booked up for first- and second-class passengers. The *Adriatic* will carry 400 first-class passengers and 500 second-class and the *Olympic* 700 and 900 respectively. These figures represent probably the largest number of cabin passengers in record to have left England for the United States, or vice versa, within one short period. First-class fares have not been increased, but a higher second-class tariff is in operation since the commencement of the war, and is likely to continue whilst there is so great a demand on the services of the liners. There is a heavy slump in third-class passage bookings between Europe and America ascribed entirely to the war.[3]

The Adelphi was packed with Americans in August 1914.

Unlike the Second World War, when Merseyside experienced substantial aerial bombardment, the region did not sustain any damage from Zeppelins or aeroplanes between 1914 and 1918. On 31 January 1916, German aircraft attempted to reach Liverpool and Birkenhead but mistook Tipton and Wednesbury in the West Midlands for the Merseyside towns. German newspapers published dramatic accounts of Liverpool and Birkenhead aflame. As seen in this account by the Irish-born American journalist, Sidney Samuel McClure, the German claims were easily refuted. Yet the desire to depict Merseyside in flames reveals how important the region was to the British war effort. Not long after the failed attempt to bomb Merseyside, a magazine for a boy scout troop based in Grove Mount, Penny Lane, offered advice on how to be prepared for Zeppelins and the black-outs that were in place as a result of the Zeppelin threat. Air-raids blurred the line between the battle front and the home front.[4] Indeed, there were some perils faced by civilians in blacked-out cities, such as crossing busy streets, which did not concern soldiers.

When I was in Berlin last February, I read accounts of the Zeppelin raids in Liverpool, Birkenhead and Manchester. The German Naval Staff issued this report on 1 February:

'One of our airship squadrons last night threw bombs over a wide area on the docks, harbours, and factories in and near Liverpool and Birkenhead ... Everywhere could be observed important results, heavy explosions, and great fires ... Our airship was violently bombarded at all points.'

The German Embassy in Washington on 24 February received the following report:

'Competent German authorities give the following details concerning the airship attack on England on the night between 31 January and 1 February. Liverpool docks and quayside factories were the principal objective. The bombs had good results, as a great fire was visible when the ship turned homewards. A large number of bridges between the docks were so severely damaged that for the present they cannot be used. In addition several ships in the Mersey were severely damaged, amongst them a cruiser, anchored below Birkenhead, and a transport steamer belonging to the Leyland line. A stable with two hundred horses was destroyed by fire, and the horses, with their Canadian stable men, are said to have perished. The Booth line and the Yeoward line suffered severely, as their docks were partly destroyed. In addition, neighbouring dry-docks and engine-works were destroyed. Birkenhead dry-dock and the engine and boiler-works completely. In all, over two hundred houses were destroyed by bombs and fires. At Bootle, at the mouth of the Mersey, a powder factory was completely destroyed.'

In Berlin I saw an article in the London 'Times' by Lord Northcliffe describing a visit to Verdun. In one place he remarked that the German official reports of the situation at Verdun were as devoid as truth as their reports of the Zeppelin raids over Liverpool and adjacent territory.

As soon as I reached Liverpool I was eager to see for myself what had happened. I saw nothing, for nothing had happened. No Zeppelin had ever come near Liverpool, Birkenhead, or Manchester. A Swedish journalist, who had made a most thorough investigation soon after the reported raid, wrote to his paper, the Stockholm 'Dagblad':

'No hostile airship has been over Liverpool or Birkenhead, or, for the matter of that, over Crewe either, a place which I visited without finding any trace of Zeppelin damage. It follows that they have not been able to cause any damage there. The authorities in Liverpool and Birkenhead – towns which, as is well known, lie on the opposite ends of the wide Mersey River – gave me all the assistance I wished. I was allowed to go wherever I wished. Among other things, one of the directors of Cammel Laird showed me over a whole of this immense shipbuilding establishment, in order that I might see with my own eyes and thus verify the facts. I saw every dock and every dry-dock in Liverpool and Birkenhead and every dock-bridge ...

'I completed my detailed investigation by making inquiries from foreigners living in Liverpool, amongst whom was the Swedish Consul, who confirmed the fact that hostile airships have never been over the town.'[5]

The Zeppelin Peril: Some useful hints and observations.

Things are looking very black in Liverpool at night time now, the reason for this being found in the precautionary measures adopted by the Authorities with regard to the reduction of lighting. Prior to the raid on the Midlands by Zeppelins at the end of January, Liverpool was considered practically immune, and accordingly the lighting regulations were not rigidly enforced. After this raid, when the possibilities of the hostile aircraft reaching Liverpool and District became greater, strict measures had to be taken, with the result that we are all developing an extra sense of being able to see in the dark.

All good scouts know that part of their training is the development of their eyes so that objects can be discerned at a good distance in the dark, so we must thank the Authorities for giving us a first rate opportunity of putting precept into practice.

There are many little risks to be encountered now that the streets are so dark, and knowledge of the rule of the road will stand everybody in good stead. If you want to cross the road or street, don't step off the pavement with your back to the direction of the oncoming traffic; always walk slightly towards the traffic, and upon reaching the middle of the road, turn half left, so that you still have your face to the direction of the traffic. A taxi, or even a cycle, moves very rapidly, and although provided with good headlights, it is very difficult for the driver or rider to see anybody in front on a dark night, until they are almost on top of them.

When on the footwalk, always remember the rule 'Keep to the Right'. If every pedestrian observed this rule, those nasty little collisions that occur so frequently would be reduced to a minimum. Don't run about in the dark, it is bad enough at the best of times, and now that it is so difficult to see ahead, there is a very good chance of your running into a lamp post, or some other hard subject [sic], with disastrous results to yourself, apart from knocking somebody over and possibly causing a nasty accident.

So much for the ordinary precautions to adopt. In the case of a visit from enemy aircraft, it is quite likely they will leave a visiting card or two in the shape of bombs, explosive and incendiary. Bombs are nasty objects and have a bad habit of exploding and causing damage. Should you happen be in the vicinity of a bomb when it drops, you drop too. By falling flat on the ground, the chances of being hit by splinters are reduced to a minimum. Don't think twice about it, but flop down right away, and, above all, keep cool. People are liable to get into a panic in the case of something out of the ordinary happening, and if you and other Scouts in the crowd would keep cool, the people would soon settle down, and be able to take the necessary precautions.[6]

Spy-fever existed before war broke out. German military and industrial spies were mentioned in the news and novels.[7] Anxiety about spies increased as Britain's position as an industrial and military power was threatened by the relatively young, scientifically astute German nation. With the start of the war, many feared that there were spies everywhere planning all kinds of carnage. As it turned out, the fear of spies could be more dangerous than the spies themselves. Below is a brief report of the inquest brought about by the shooting of a pedlar by a sentry. There was little sympathy for the pedlar whose insistence on carrying on his way cost him his life. The second example of spy-fever on Merseyside is comic rather than tragic, but with one false move the incident could have turned out very differently.

The circumstances under which a pedlar named William Robert Dawson (62) was shot by a sentry at Dunning's Bridge, Maghull, were explained before Mr Coroner Brighouse, yesterday, when he held an inquest on the unfortunate man at Maghull.

Evidence was given to the effect that the deceased, who was a single man and had no fixed abode, was late on Tuesday night observed by a sentry on duty at the bridge to be proceeding in the direction of Liverpool. He was challenged by the sentry, who called upon him three times to halt. The deceased, however, did not reply, whereupon the sentry ordered him to put up his hands. The man replied 'To – with you and hands up,' and the sentry fired, the deceased immediately falling. He was taken to the Maghull Epileptic Home nearby, where he expired shortly after.

The Coroner said it was absolutely essential in the interests of the community that certain acts at these times must be performed by the military, and individuals must sink their individuality for the benefit of the community of which they were part. By walking along the highway at midnight at present a man, speaking vulgarly, was 'asking for it,' and the question for the jury to consider was whether the soldier in good faith had reasonable grounds in the interests of the State to justify what he did.[8]

A spy story with an amusing ending originates from Birkenhead.

The other night several special constables were returning from drill, and when in the neighbourhood of Higher Tranmere their attention was attracted to four men who, armed with lamps, were walking along the housetops.

After watching the men for a few minutes the 'specials' decided that they were spies, and that they were making signals to some unknown enemy. An order was given, and in a few seconds the houses were surrounded. The men on the roof were then summarily ordered to descend or suffer dire penalties.

Much to the astonishment of the special constables the order was complied with quite meekly. When the men reached the ground it was seen that the lights consisted of bicycle lamps. The explanation of their movements was quite simple; they had been searching for a leak.[9]

Very few people are aware of the Bootle corned beef scandal of 1916. While it does not occupy the same place in the history books as the shell scandal of the previous year, it does point toward the fundamental question of food and its availability on the home front. In this case the secretary of the Liverpool Labour Representation Committee, Fred Hoey, informs the secretary of the National Labour Party about an example of food being brought over to the country, stored and then shipped out again. Although there were no significant food shortages in 1916, some politicians were keeping an eye on wastage and the availability of food in working-class constituencies. In the House of Commons on 10 August 1916, G. Faber, MP for Battersea and Clapham, argued 'that already meat is passing outside the purchasing power of great numbers of the people of this country'.[10] The situation improved when more British meat came available later in the year, but during August 1916 Hoey, Faber and others were apprehensive about the welfare of the working classes.[11]

27 Aug 1916

Dear Sir and Bro.

I have been supplied with reliable information, through the Warehouse Workers' Union, that 1450 cases of Canadian corned beef arrived in this city 2 years ago (Mark MS/4). They were stored at L + N W Railway Company warehouses, Alexandra Dock, Bootle.

On 24 August 1916 the same 1450 cases were carted down to SS *Metagama* + loaded on board. The same mark is on the cases. The *Metagama* sailed on Thursday for Canada with the beef.

This may form a basis for a question (say by Bro. W. Anderson)

'Will the Government enquire whether the SS *Metagama* sailed from Liverpool on Thursday 24 August 1916 with 1450 cases of Canadian corned beef, mark MS/4, the same having been imported from Canada 2 years ago, stored in L + N W Railway Co. Warehouses, Alexandra Dock, Bootle, + now re-shipped to Canada with the apparent object of being sold to H M Government at an increased price, and will they take drastic action in cases such as this to prevent the transference of food stuff from England where it is alleged there is a shortage.'[12]

By the end of 1917, food shortages had become more common. In 1917, a German submarine blockade contributed to the scarcity of some items, and a food controller, Lord Devonport, was appointed in 1916. Rationing took place on a local and then on a national scale from July 1918. In January 1918, the rationing of butter, margarine and tea was introduced by the Liverpool Food Committee. As the following report in the *Evening Express* shows, some businesses decided to ration before decisions were taken by local or national authorities. Bread was not rationed during the war, although the Wheat Commission did stress the importance of limiting the amount eaten and reducing wastage.[13] In February 1918, twenty tons of potatoes, specially prepared for making bread, were being delivered every day to Liverpool bakers.[14]

It is admitted that there is a world food shortage, but up to now this country has escaped that degree of severity which has been felt in other countries. At the moment the pinch is being felt with regard to tea. There are wild rumours of a serious tea shortage, but an 'Express' representative was authoritatively informed to-day that what shortage there is is only temporary and 'unless the public follows the lead of the hoarders and goes insane, it will be over in a week or two.'

The fact, nevertheless, remains that in certain shops in Liverpool, as in other parts of the country, tradesmen are unable to satisfy the public demand. The Liverpool City Co-operative Society has inaugurated rationing with a combined tea and sugar card, and members will only be supplied with half a pound of tea and their usual amount of sugar per week.

At Liverpool stores there was found very little China tea on sale at 3s, and only a small amount of Government controlled tea. 'We have been compelled,' said the manager, 'to limit our serve to half a pound per customer. We only do this in the interests of the public. I am quite satisfied that some miserable people are hoarding, and in doing so they are playing a very unpatriotic and selfish game. I would like to have a way discovered of penalising them. The present shortage, which is due almost entirely to the actions of these people, will be only temporary. As a matter of fact, the Government have promised that the situation will be very much easier by the end of October, or at the very latest by the beginning of November.'

Some shops in Liverpool are selling tea at 4s and 4s 6d per lb. But this is not so bad as in London ...

Other foodstuffs have a tendency to be scarce, with high prices. Butter is at almost famine prices and very hard to get, and bacon similarly is scarce and dear although the quality has greatly improved. There is no Danish bacon to be had in Liverpool to-day. The only supply, and that is a limited one, is American, which is being sold at 2s 2d per lb. This same quality of bacon fifteen years ago could have been bought in England at 3d per lb. and less.

Semi-official statements have made it fairly clear that we must expect a dearth of bacon, butter, and margarine as a repercussion of the Anglo-American commercial restrictions now imposed in Denmark and Holland ... Our Government (writes a correspondent) are holding up ships and supplies, and while we do that we cannot expect to get much traffic in the other direction. The Americans are to supply us with more butter and bacon in order to meet the deficiency.

By the Currants and Sultanas (Requisition) Order, 1917, the Food Controller takes over all currents and sultanas now afloat and shipped to the United Kingdom. The price to be paid by the Food Controller is left over to subsequent destination.

All persons owning or having power to sell or dispose of any such currants and sultanas are required, before October 20th, to furnish to the Secretary, Ministry of Food, Grosvenor House, WI, returns showing quantities of such currants and sultanas now afloat, setting out in each case the quantities sold and unsold.[15]

Feeding the nation: a chicken run in Walton. (Courtesy of Liverpool Record Office, Liverpool Libraries 352 ENG/2/3275)

Although the cost and availability of food was a widely acknowledged problem, it is easy to overlook the challenge raised by the disposal of waste. There may well have been not as many men in the city than there had been before the war, but that also meant that there were fewer men to collect the waste. With more than half of the staff having joined the military, it was going to be difficult to keep the streets clean. Moreover, many of the recent wartime appointments were deemed inferior to the men who they replaced. One way around the shortage was to employ women in some roles, such as sweeping the street. The observation about waste not being incinerated may owe as much to the cost of coal during the war or compliance with Board of Trade Coal economy campaigns as carelessness.

The Health Committee report that in normal times a weekly collection of the contents of ... bins is given in Liverpool, and in a number of especially large houses it has been found necessary to give a more frequent collection, averaging about twice a week.

The capacity of the Corporation Standard Bin amounts to about 2 ¾ cubic feet, and in practice this is found to hold the refuse for a period of two weeks from a small house where care is exercised.

The bins were, as originally reported to the Committee, made of this size because it was felt desirable to provide an ample margin as the volume of refuse varies according to the season, and such a bin when full, though requiring a strong man to work it, could be handled economically by one man.

Since the commencement of the war, and particularly during the winter months, round about the Christmas and New Year Holidays, special difficulty has been found in dealing with certain areas where the quantity of ashes and refuse made has been much greater than usual. In many cases material found in the bin has only been partially burnt, and undoubtedly care has not been exercised in seeing that combustible material, such as half-burnt coal, paper and cardboard and vegetable matter, has been fully utilised in the fire-grates.

The custom in the Department is to record the emptying of every bin, and records can, if necessary, be turned up showing the date on which each bin or ash pit in the City was emptied.

An inspection of these returns shows that round about the Christmas and New Year Holiday time, owing to the class and number of men available for this work, the collection had to some extent fallen behind, but the Department has, as far as possible, given a fortnightly collection, though in some cases a longer interval has elapsed.

The situation is very much improved, and bins are now receiving attention once a fortnight. With a fortnightly collection there is no excuse for depositing in the passages, and steps will be taken to prosecute in cases where deposits are made. It should be pointed out that every man who has presented himself for work during the past 10 or 12 weeks has been employed, though in the majority of cases they have not stayed more than two or three days at work.

Women street cleaners filling a gap in the workforce. (Courtesy of Liverpool Record Office, Liverpool Libraries 352 ENG/2/3031)

Out of an approximate staff of 900 men, 465, or over 50 per cent, have joined the colours.

At the present time there are engaged in the Cleansing Department 580 men. The men who have replaced those absent are not equal as workmen to the regular bin hands.[16]

In a thoughtful twelve-page essay, *The War its Unseen Cause and Some of its Lessons*, Joseph Bibby suggests some unconventional reasons for the outbreak of the war. The founder of J. Bibby and Sons, seed crushers, Justice of the Peace for the City of Liverpool and Councillor for Exchange Ward, Liverpool, thought that the war was the result of karmic forces. While he did place the blame on Germany, he saw the origins of the war in the negative thoughts and actions that were present throughout Western Europe in the Edwardian era. In Britain all the bad feeling in Ireland, the class tension and the militant action by the suffragettes led to a hostile atmosphere that played a part in bringing about the war. Bibby was a theosophist who believed that modern societies lacked unity and were riddled with divides founded on class and property. He hoped that the war would help unite people. Yet the essay was published in 1915 so it is likely that Bibby would have been disappointed by the class divides that came to the fore later in the war and during the inter-war years.

'[W]e should form the good habit of always looking out for the good points in everyone we should meet; and especially should we seek out the good qualities in those whom we find it most difficult to get along with. With such thoughts in mind, let us, first of all, study in a spirit of fairness the life and character of our so-called enemy, the German nation; peradventure, we may come into some sort of sympathetic relationship with the people of that country and then understand how two so-called civilised peoples should find themselves in deadly conflict, when neither of them has any real advantage to gain from the injury they are trying to inflict on each other ... I think the outstanding feature of the German social life, as compared with our own or that of the Belgians or French, is that the German national spirit is stronger and more united than it is with us; this spirit, which we may call nationalism pervades the whole nation from the Kaiser downwards ... She [Germany] is placed in that unfortunate position that she desired colonies for her overflow population, and has come too late; the world is already parcelled out ...

All wrong doing in the world is a result of the deflection of the judgement by the *bias of self-seeking desire*. Had Germany been cultivating the habit of desiring to seek her own good through service to others, which is the true path of advancement, she would never have made the choice she did when she hastily embarked upon war, seeing that none of her real interests were threatened.

The War, as I read its meaning, is a great crisis in the life of our nation; it is alike the harvest of our past sowing and the sowing time for the next harvest, and the same may be said of all the other nations concerned. If you ask the 'Man in the street' why we are suffering the enormous losses incurred by the war, he will tell you that it is caused entirely by the Germans ... But the truth must be stated that this loss and suffering has come upon us in a way we could not honourably avoid; it was evidently in part of our Karma; we have sown the seed, and we must reap the crop ...

Cannot we trace here a direct connection between our having to participate in the war on the Continent and the intolerant thoughts which we have been so freely putting in the atmosphere in Ireland; for did not the German Ambassador advise the Berlin Chancellor that, so far as he could see, we were on the very brink of civil war? There does not appear to be the slightest doubt that this report encouraged Germany to choose the present moment to make her mad attack on France and trample upon Belgium, thinking, no doubt, that we should have enough to do with our own domestic troubles, without taking a hand in other peoples' quarrels ...

[W]e have been charging our mental atmosphere with the most appropriate medium for the rapid increase and multiplication of the war bacillus.[17]

The author of this letter had a problem with the working classes who had not joined the army or navy and whose wages had increased during the war. As a ship owner and member of the Mersey Dock Board, J. H. Beazley was particularly upset by the dock workers, who he thought were not doing enough to clear the build-up of goods at the port. The opinions of leading businessmen like Bibby and Beazley were more often recorded than those of the workers. What is more, they were individuals and the workers were a diverse group who did not hold a single opinion about the war and their part in it. In an effort to resolve the problem of congestion at the port, a Liverpool Dock Battalion was formed in March 1915. Members of the battalion would be available at all times, wore uniform and received a guaranteed minimum wage. Other dock workers were unhappy with the battalion because they feared it would pave the way for the conscription of labour.[18] The second, anonymous letter is less even less diplomatic than Beazley's censure of the dock workers.

Sir, It is very disturbing to learn from the daily papers how the working classes – i.e. such as have not joined his Majesty's forces – are behaving in the present crisis. Whilst the bulk of the community is doing all that lies in their power to help their country, the working classes seem to be exploiting the war by wringing extra wages out of their employers (over and above advances already given) much beyond what the circumstances justify.

Take the dockers, for instance, their wages are higher now than they have ever been, but instead of reciprocating by giving their best and steadiest work, many of them will not give a full week's work, but prefer to loaf and amuse themselves during half the week, although they are urgently needed to discharge and load the vessels that are waiting. Recently scores of men might have been seen along the line of the docks playing 'pitch and toss,' and declining to work when called upon.

Then again, 10,000 men on the Clyde are out on strike, though they know very well that it is of the most vital importance that work in the shipbuilding and engineering yards should be pushed on with the greatest possible despatch, but, no, they think only of their own selfish interests and let their country 'go hang.'

There are other classes of workmen pursuing the same line of unpatriotic conduct, who, instead of doing all they possibly can to help the successful perpetuation of the great fight forced upon us, are thinking only of their own selfish interests and making no special efforts whatever, their only contribution to the common good being their trifling payments in the extra tea and beer duties.

All this is not as it should be, and it is deplorable that the working men of the country – other than those who have joined the colours – are not rising to the occasion by putting patriotism before self and doing their utmost to help in the time of need. Surely their leaders, if they are true leaders ought to teach them the way.

In contradistinction to this, how different are other classes of the community behaving. Take the clerks and shop assistants, for instance. They are giving their best – working long hours without extra remuneration in order, as far as lies in their powers, to fill the gaps caused by many of their number having gone to fight their country's battles, and they very properly and patriotically look upon this as their contribution to their county's weal.

Again, how many thousands all over the country are helping in the numerous hospitals, permanent and temporary (many of the latter of which have been fitted up and given free), whilst others are assisting the various organisations established to help the dependants of those who are fighting our battles on land and sea, giving their services without fee or rewards and being content with the knowledge that they are doing their duty to their country in its hour of need. Perhaps the working classes do not yet realise how much is at stake in this struggle and how much even their interests – more than those of any other class – would be seriously affected by a failure to overcome German domination now? How unfair and prejudicial their present conduct is to those who are bravely fighting our battles at the front. I think it is a pity that our statesmen on both sides don't speak throughout the country and explain frankly that this war is one of life and death for us.

Yours, J. H. Beazley, Liverpool, 25 February 1915.[19]

Sir, The other morning troopships were disembarking gallant Canadian troops. These men have volunteered and come over to this country to fight for us.

Watching the landing were scores of well-dressed, healthy young strikers, all of military age, with a well cared for and contented expression.

What are the authorities doing to allow this state of things to exist a single hour when the country is supposed to be passing through the crisis of the war?

Disgusted.[20]

It is difficult to pinpoint what motivated William Beaman's public criticism of Lord Derby and Lord Kitchener. One possible reason for Beaman's outburst may have been the formation of Lord Derby's Dock Battalion. Lord Kitchener had given Derby permission to organise the battalion on military lines. At the time there was talk about the 'conscription of labour'. To increase production, some argued, it would be necessary to curtail to power of labour. Like many trade unionists, Beaman may have feared that the Dock Battalion was the start of a movement that would see workers in key industries being treated like a branch of the military.

For disorderly conduct – making remarks which caused a disturbance – William Henry Beaman, Clifton-street, Garston, was fined 20s or eleven days imprisonment at the local court to-day, by Alderman Dart and Mr A. E. Jacob.

Plain-clothes officer Roberts said Beaman was using bad language in Chapel-road, Garston, and making rude remarks about Lord Derby and Lord Kitchener, which created a disturbance.

When witness got him home he was still very disorderly and cried, 'Let me get my gun and I will blow their brains out.'

Defendant did not appear, and his wife said that he was working for the Government on explosive work. He was very sorry for his conduct.[21]

In April 1917 the Military Service (Review of Exceptions) Act was passed. To make up for the scarcity of troops, the act called on military tribunals to re-examine men under thirty-one who were previously deemed unsuitable for front line service and those

North Haymarket Munitions Factory, Liverpool, 22 June 1915. (Courtesy of Liverpool Record Office, Liverpool Libraries 352 ENG/2/3001)

who had left the army. To challenge this legislation, James Hogge set up the National Federation of Discharged and Demobilised Sailors and Soldiers. The Federation put up a candidate, Frank Hughes, to contest a Liverpool seat against Lord Stanley, eldest son of the Secretary of State for War and founder of the Liverpool Dock Battalion, Lord Derby. A great deal of attention was paid to the contest. Although Lord Stanley won the by-election, the government amended the legislation so that disabled ex-service men would not be re-examined. This report captures some of the excitement as government ministers were challenged by men who had been discharged from the army and awarded the Silver Badge.

The 'Silver badge' election at Liverpool is being contested with vigour, and the result is regarded as being very open. Mr Hughes, the nominee of the discharged soldiers and sailors, is expected to run a close fight with Lord Derby's son.

There is a nominal electorate of 6,028, but the register is completely out of date, and a large number of electors are in the Army and Navy, and will not be able to vote. A 60 per cent poll is the best that can be hoped for, or a total of about 3,600. The numerical strength of the dissentients is not known with any precision, but if it should reach, say, 1,500, the margin of safety will be too narrow to warrant undue confidence on the part of Lord Stanley's supporters.

On the subject of the Irish vote in the contest we have received the following letter from Mr J. P. Byrne, chairman of the Manchester and Salford District Committee of the United Irish League:

'Sir, The statement that the United Irish League in the Abercromby Division of Liverpool was supporting Lord Stanley having appeared in the Manchester press, permits me to officially contradict the same. It is not true. J. P. Byrne.'

Mr Macpherson, the Under-Secretary for War, was vigorously heckled by discharged soldiers at last night's meeting in Hope Hall, but he gave a good account of himself.

At one point he was dramatically challenged by a man who said that he had been discharged because of a poisoned stomach contracted in a dugout at Ypres, and yet had recently been called up again.

'Then don't go,' said Mr Macpherson.

'But will you sign this paper?' asked the ex-soldier. 'Certainly,' was the reply, and the document was at once signed by Mr Macpherson, cancelling the call.

It was a monstrous scandal, added the speaker, to say that the graves of the honoured dead in France were neglected, and it was iniquitous to exploit wounded soldiers and put them out to the highest bidder.

A telegram this afternoon states that both sides are vigorously at work. The Unionists had no public meetings to-day, except those in the open air. Mr Hughes' supporters addressed outdoor gatherings, at which the candidate himself spoke.

Mr Hogge MP, intimated his intention to reply to Mr Macpherson's Liverpool speech tonight at Mr Hughes' meetings, at which Sir Godfrey Baring, Mr Pringle, and Mr Harry Watt are announced to speak.

The Unionists have arranged a meeting for to-night, at which the principal speaker will be Mr G. H. Roberts, Parliamentary Secretary of the Board of Trade.[22]

Fred Bower did not want a world war, he wanted a revolution. In his autobiography, *Rolling Stonemason*, Bower set out his view of the war. As an international socialist, Bower divided the world into the exploiters and the exploited. He moved from Boston, USA, to Liverpool with his parents and became a stonemason. He became involved in syndicalism and penned the infamous leaflet 'Don't Shoot' (1912) that called on soldiers not to fire on strikers. The leaflet resulted in the arrest of Bower along with other radicals under the Incitement to Mutiny Act (1797). During the war, Bower assisted others who opposed the conflict. He described one notable example in the extract below. However, his attempt to help the crippled escapee (Ferdinand Louis Kerhan) failed. A steward on the ship recognised the escaped prisoner, who was returned to Britain where he was put on trial in Liverpool and sent back to prison.

Right at the beginning of the war, I had made up my mind that the powers that be would not get me to kill a man. They could gaol or kill me, as they had the power, but I knew that it was not the workers' fight. Being born in a country does not make that country a man's possession, any more than being born in a certain house makes that house the property of the person born in it ...

[I]n the early days of the war our meetings were dispersed, and the speakers rough-handled. It was: Believe what Bottomley, and Lloyd George, and the *Daily Mail* say, or be damned! It is not too hard to be a parrot, and repeat what your masters and pastors tell you, and so, when they and the gutter press said that Ramsay MacDonald, and Snowden, and those who supported them in their views were enemies of England, there were always plenty of half-insane 'patriotic' hooligans to show their bravery by smashing up honest (even if deluded) speakers' meetings, in between riffling German butchers' shops.

In Liverpool, I found the shipping companies were stuck for men to man their ships, in the firing and stewarding departments. Many Quakers and honest conscientious objectors were supplied with bogus birth certificates, and discharges, and shipped on as firemen. Some stuck to the job whilst the war lasted, some cleared off in American ports. I can only think the authorities winked at the proceedings, for their sleuths must have known it was going on. And, in any case, the shipping companies got their firemen ...

The cripple [who had escaped from prison after being interned for leading 'Stop the War' meetings] came disguised to Liverpool. I saw his photograph in a current copy of the *Mirror*, and a few hours after met him. I penetrated his disguise. There was a reward of £100 for his arrest. Going up to him, I put my arm on his shoulder and said: 'I arrest you for escaping gaol'. He blanched, but I put him out of his misery by winking. Taking him home, I rigged him in old sea gear. He was an artist, and proud of his long hair and clean hands. When I had cropped his hair as close to the scalp as I could and rubbed charcoal into his finger nails, his mother wouldn't have known him. He almost cried as he surveyed himself in the glass. Getting another chap to sign on under the name of Farrell, we passed the signing-on note to the cripple. 'Now,' I said, 'forget your Oxford accent, and do a bit of bloodying, or the regular men will tumble.' So I took him aboard the boat on which he was to be a fireman, the S.S. *Scythia*. He was a man who hadn't lifted anything heavier than a camera in his life, and I thought to myself: 'God help you, mate. You'll know what work is soon.'[23]

A debate about electoral reform in Liverpool in April 1918 resulted in a depopulated council chamber as Irish Nationalists, Labour and many Liberal members walked out in protest. The following summary from the *Liverpool, Bootle, Birkenhead and Wallasey Official Red Book* summarises a heated meeting that reverberated throughout the city. The experiment would have involved the city's eleven electoral divisions being replaced by two areas, North and South Liverpool, with five and six members respectively. Among the reasons why the Conservatives were so opposed was the potential

Fred Bower was opposed
to the war. (Author's collection)

cost of the experiment, and the business vote would be cancelled out for those men who lived in the same area as their business. The Conservatives also objected to the idea of a significant city like Liverpool being the subject of a political experiment. Liverpool's Conservatives challenged the government to be bold and apply it everywhere or not bother at all. Others, though, felt that Liverpool's minorities were not duly represented by the existing system.[24]

April 4 – Special Meeting to consider question of proportional representation, Lord Mayor Utting presiding. The Labour Party entered a protest against the terms of the proposed resolution not being printed, but this was over-ruled. Ald. Sir A. Salvidge moved and Ald. Burgess seconded a resolution against the selection of Liverpool for experimenting with proportional representation. Ald. Harford objected to the way the matter had been brought forward and left the Council Chamber, followed by the rest of the Nationalist members. Mr W. A. Robinson having remarked that the Labour Party favoured proportional representation, he and the other Labour members walked out. During Ald. Burgesses' [sic] speech, most of the Liberal Councillors withdrew although Sir W. Forwood appealed to members to remain. In the result the resolution was carried nem. dis. [no one dissenting] after brief

Sir John Utting, Lord Mayor of Liverpool
1918–19. (Author's collection)

discussion, by the votes of the Conservatives, there being none of the opposition left. [25]

This account of a fight between discharged soldiers reflects the humorous tone of some local newspaper report. At the same time, it sheds light on the domestic problems that continued irrespective of whether or not there was a war. In fact, the war could accentuate some domestic or family trouble. It appears that Cullet heard about Collins' aggressive behaviour towards his sister after his young brother came back from sea. Cullet appears to have taken on the responsibility for looking after his siblings and felt a duty to defend his sister. Although it is not clear from this report, it is possible that Cullet's sister had formed another relationship while her husband was away. The war could accentuate any pre-existing tensions in a relationship. Collins was not the only soldier to find that his wife had moved on. The second source is a piece that related the story of a far gentler soldier whose wife fell pregnant after a brief affair with his brother. While this story may have been the product of the journalist's vivid imagination, it does indicate that there was apprehension about the fate of those who came back to find themselves in anything but a perfect marriage.

Woolton has had its battle front, and a goodly crowd on Sunday afternoon week watched a struggle between two discharged soldiers, Andrew Cullet (31), of 26 Rose street, and Frederick Collins (27), of 5, Rose Bank, Rose street. Evidently a decisive victory was not achieved, for the parties were still unreconciled when they met at the Woolton Police Court on Friday, before Mr T. J. McGeorge, to answer the charge of fighting.

Police-Constable Stewart said that at 3.50 on Sunday afternoon, the 28th ult., Cullet and Collins were fighting in Rose Street. They had their coats and vests off, and were punching each other with their fists. He separated them, and saw Collins home. He was bleeding from the mouth. Both men were sober.

Cullet said that Collins was looking for bother. Collins married his youngest sister. On the Sunday morning his young brother had come from sea, and had been in a convoy. He heard that Collins was thrashing his sister, and he could not stand there and see him hit her. 'I think it was up to me to stop a thing like that.'

Collins said he was having his dinner. His wife had been down Hillfoot, and as he did not think that was a respectable place for a married woman to go so he remonstrated with her. Cullen came to the top of the street, and said 'You may as well hit me as hit your wife,' and he then struck him without any provocation. His wife had been away since Tuesday, and had left the children. That was the way she was carrying on. He had no luck since he had been in the family. He wished the magistrates would give him a separation. He would keep the children, and he had a good discharge from the Army.

The magistrates said the defendants ought not to take the law into their own hands.

Cullet: People in the street called me a coward to stand there and see my sister hit. She is only a little woman, and you can see how big he is.

Inspector Jones said that Collins had been 14 times and Cullet 12 times before the magistrates.

They were each fined 20s., the magistrates remarking that they had no right to make the public street the place for their quarrels.[26]

Mr H. G. Wells and other prominent publicists are agitating for a reform of our divorce law and in view of their arguments the following story, which a Liverpool soldier related to the writer as to his recent homecoming from 'Somewhere in France' has a telling and pathetic significance.

'At last I got ten days' leave. I had volunteered soon after the outbreak of war, for I felt the country needed all the men she could get, and, also that our cause was a righteous one. After the usual training I was at last despatched with my regiment abroad, and had spent the last eighteen months "Somewhere in France." A great portion of the time had been spent in the fighting line, and thus I knew what it was to be in Hell. But my thoughts and my dreams were chiefly about my home – my wife and my two little ones. And now at last I had got ten days' leave. How sweet the thought of home, and the joy I should experience in being once more in the presence of my loved ones!

'Eventually I reached home. But, alas, when I reached it, it was to me a home no longer. All my thoughts and my dreams were shattered in a moment. It is true the house was there, and so was my wife and my two little ones; but, in addition, there was a baby, only three weeks' old, in my wife's arms.

'I was thunderstruck. What was the meaning of it? I demanded the story from her. After many tears she told me. It appears that my brother, whom I had not seen for some years, and who was a sailor, came last Xmas and spent several days in my house carousing and making love to my wife, and then went off to sea again. Even he does not know the result of their intimacy. What could I do?

'I went and consulted a magistrate's clerk and laid the particulars of the case before him, and asked for a "separation." He told me what the law was – that I could get no separation order, but that the law would eventually release me from my wife if I took divorce proceedings. But it was not only expensive; it would take some time. If I wished I could proceed "in forma pauperis," i.e. get a poor man's divorce, but that might cost £20 as well as take some time. But I had no £20. He said I could, if I wished, in the meantime arrange to have my wife's army allowance stopped.

'I was in a dilemma and was heartbroken. Time was short. Who was to look after my two little children? And what was to become of my wife and her little one if the army allowance was stopped? I have gone back to "Somewhere in France." But what are my thoughts and my dreams now?'[27]

In 1919 race riots broke out in Britain, with the worst disturbances taking place in Liverpool and Cardiff. Black war workers and soldiers were targeted, along with other minorities. The spark for the riots came from anger at interracial relationships. This report from a popular Liverpool newspaper two years before the disturbances took place gives some idea of attitudes to migrants from Africa. Under the heading 'Black and White: Negroes marrying Liverpool Girls', the *Evening Express* 'special' report opens with a description of a black man and white woman meeting. The first half of the report reads like a script for a play, thus allowing the author to elaborate on the appearance and behaviour of the couple. The final part of the tableau, as they disappear from sight behind the foliage, leaves the reader to conjecture as to what the pair will be doing in that secluded spot. As Lucy Bland has argued, there was not simply one type of racism during the Edwardian period. In fact, there were some who complimented the migrants.[28] Indeed, a combination of condemnation and praise can be seen in this report, along with a fair amount of envy.

Scene: Princes Boulevard, Liverpool.
    Time: Eight o'clock, a few days ago. A lovely summer evening.
    A negro elegantly – one might almost say gloriously – attired, is standing in a graceful pose, apparently aimlessly watching the traffic. A straw hat gaily ribboned, is rakishly tilted on his head. His suit is a fine advertisement for his tailor and a bright coloured tie with loose ends flies open at his breast affording occasional glimpses of a pure white shirt. Smart creased pants and patent leather shoes which do not quite conceal his delicately tinted socks complete the picture. He takes a handsome gold watch from his pocket, sees the time, and begins to stroll slowly along.

At this very moment there emerges from a house in one of the streets running off the Avenue a neatly-attired girlish figure. Here is a vision of English maidenly beauty. The girl immediately sees the negro a dozen yards away. She trips right along to greet him, her face suffused with blushes. He raises his hat, and his broad lips part to disclose one of the most beautiful of human charms, a row of perfect white teeth.

'You are up to time I see.' She exclaims.

'Oh, rather!' is the ecstatic reply.

And the two walk off into the park and soon the beautiful foliage of the trees hides the happy pair from view.

It is an alliance of black and white. And it affords an illustration of many such alliances which are taking place in Liverpool just now.

There is probably no more cosmopolitan city in the world than Liverpool, as many nationalities have their colours dotted here and there about the city. The negro element has never been regarded as a strong one. But a great change has come over the scene. Negros in ever-increasing numbers are arriving at the port and settling down here. They are finding that work is plentiful and the wages are good, and they are sending word to their friends on the West Coast of Africa to follow their example. To obtain work at the docks, in the munitions factories, and in the sugar refineries, and for the most part they are proving good citizens. They are civil and well behaved and no particular exception is being taken to their presence in our midst.

It is only necessary to take a step in the direction of Park-road and Stanley-street to see how completely the negro colony has dug itself in, to use a battlefield term. Where in the old days one or two loafing niggers were to be seen, they are to-day to be met in droves. And it must be said they add to the picturesqueness of the life of the district. Always brightly and very often expensively dressed, they have brought a colour to a district which would otherwise be aptly described as drab. But they display an air of prosperity and affluence which was not apparent in their other days only a few years ago. They are to be seen occasionally riding bicycles of expensive make, they are usually smoking cigars and appear to have a good deal of time on their hands.[29]

Princes Road: a place to be seen. (Author's collection)

Two slices of bread caused quite a stir in St Helens during November 1917. A workman was accused of stealing the bread from a co-worker and the case ended up before the police court. A number of aspects of this case merit attention: the spate of thefts in the rolling mills; the relationship between the three workers referred to in the report; the reason why the prisoner's wealth was assumed to absolve him of the crime; and whether the fact that the sole witness to this theft being a 'coloured man' had any bearing on the bench's decision. The bizarre affair took place at a time when the price of food was of particular concern in the country at large. Despite working a lengthy shift, the furnace man only had bread to sustain him. The absence of cheese or meat is probably a reflection of the cost of maintaining a family at this time. Whoever stole the food was either hungry or spiteful.

A wealthy workman charged with theft.

At the Police Court on Monday, before Mr T. Edmondson (in the chair), Councillor J. R. Turner and Councillor E. W. Swift, John

Halewood, a copper piecer, of 343 Eltonhead-road, was charged with stealing two pieces of bread and butter, value 3*d*, the property of Thomas Watkinson to which he pleaded not guilty.

The Chief Constable said the prosecutor resided at 14 Brook-street, and was a furnace man employed by Messrs Barton and Son, Sutton Rolling Mills, and prisoner was employed there as a copper piecer. On Thursday afternoon last the prosecutor left his position at work, and had to pass the place where the prisoner was employed. Before going he saw his dinner basket on a form [a narrow bench] in the furnace room, and it contained two pieces of bread and butter. At the rear of the furnace there was a workman named John Williams, who said that, after the prosecutor had gone away, prisoner left his place and went cautiously to the form. After looking round to see that the road was clear, he dived into the basket, took the bread and butter and ate it. Williams asked why he had taken it and he said it was his mates and he had told him to take it. When prosecutor returned Williams told him what had happened, and on examining the basket found the two pieces of bread and butter had been taken. Prosecutor accused the prisoner of having taken it, and he denied it. On the following day the prosecutor found Williams and the prisoner having an argument about it, and went between them. Prisoner said 'How would it be if Williams had taken it and is trying to blame me.' The matter was reported to the manager, and in consequence of so many thefts of this sort lately it was reported to the police, and the prisoner was arrested. When the evidence was put before them, they would find it was about as mean a theft as ever came into the court. The only food the prosecutor had to last him for eighteen hours were several pieces of dry toast and when he [the prisoner] was searched by the police, documents were found in his possession which showed that he had £671 13*s* 1*d* to his credit. He was a single man, and the prosecutor was a married man with a family.

John Williams, a coloured man, gave evidence in support of the Chief Constable's statement.

Inspector Andrews gave evidence as for the prisoner's arrest, and said that this year he had saved £194 apart from the money he had invested.

He was a single man with no dependents. He paid 4s a week for his bed and kept himself.

Prisoner said he had never touched the basket or the bread.

The Bench dismissed the case.[30]

In his *Report on the Police Establishment and the state of Crime* for 1918, Liverpool's head constable, Francis Caldwell, reflected on the war's effect on the city's police force. The force was stretched as men left to join the army at a time when the police needed to enforce more legal regulations. One of the most significant of these rules involved the registration of alien seamen. This was particularly important in a busy port. Caldwell, who was born in Liverpool, was proud of the city's role in developing an effective means to monitor alien seamen. The police also played a significant role in protecting property and lives during the *Lusitania* riots in 1915. With a police strike to come in 1919, Caldwell had busy times ahead before he stepped down in 1925, at the age of sixty-five.

A considerable number of ceremonial reviews of troops, such as those by H.M. the King, the late Lord Kitchener, the review of American Troops etc., were held, these naturally entailed a large amount of extra police duty.

The arrival of American Troops, and the presence in the City of large bodies of troops and the crews of the transports, caused much extra work and at times called for great tact and forbearance …

The greatest volume of police War Work … was that of a restrictive nature, emergency legislation and the regulations under D.O.R.A. were wide and far reaching including National Registration, Registration of Aliens, Liquor Control, Food Control, Lighting Restrictions, Motor Car Restrictions, and innumerable other restrictive orders. These regulations were so frequently issued and so constantly varied, that it was difficult to educate the public as to what they might or might not do, and exceedingly difficult for the police to see that the numerous orders which were detailed to them for enforcement were duly obeyed.

The War caused the formation of two new departments in the Force viz.: The Special Branch of the Detective Department and the Aliens' Registration department ...

All the Alien enemies about whom any doubt was felt were promptly interned soon after the outbreak of War, but with the development of the submarine campaign a new factor arose. Such terrible outrages as the sinking of the 'Lusitania' caused ebullition of public feeling first openly manifested in Liverpool where many of the victims resided, and developed into unreasoning attacks upon property which was not always that of alien enemies ...

Until 1916 when all aliens, friends as well as enemies, were required to register throughout the country, whether living in prohibited areas or non-prohibited areas, there was the danger of alien enemies coming here posing as alien friends, and to meet this a very strict supervision was kept on hotels, boarding houses, etc., and arrangements were made for dealing promptly with all suspects. With the extension of alien registration to non-prohibited areas this danger was considerably reduced as the police in non-prohibited areas were thus able to test the bona-fides of all aliens ...

To deal with the seamen it was decided in 1915 to take special measures. In conjunction with H.M. Superintending Aliens' Officer at this port, all alien seamen were carefully examined, and when proved satisfactory a special registration card with photograph and finger print was issued, and the production of this card was required by the Board of Trade before an alien could be paid off and could sign on a ship. This system when developed proved to be very efficacious, and dozens of doubtful aliens who were handed over for investigation to the Special Branch of the Detective Department proved to be alien enemies. The results obtained were so satisfactory that some six months after its inception at Liverpool it was adopted by the Home Office for use at all principal ports ...

The Women Patrols of the National Union of Women Workers did and are still doing exceedingly useful work amongst women and young girls in the streets, and in the neighbourhood of Military Camps, &c. Although their work strictly speaking may be regarded as social rescue and preventative work and outside the scope of ordinary police duty, in carrying it out they rendered much valuable assistance to the regular police …[31]

The war affected everybody in one way or another and people wanted to know what had happened, what was happening and what would come to pass. As a result fortune-tellers and those who claimed to contact the dead were in special demand during the war. This prompted Ernest William Barnes, who became a canon at Westminster Abbey in 1918, to expose the fallacies of spiritualism. Part of a series of books published by the Liverpool Diocesan Board of Divinity, *Spiritualism and the Christian Faith*, approached the subject in a rational and balanced manner. Barnes, who had given a lecture on the subject in Liverpool, had studied mathematics at Cambridge and had considered a career as an academic. Yet he does not dismiss the phenomenon out of hand. Indeed, he demonstrates a firm belief in telepathy. The second extract is a report about a Liverpool woman who falls foul of the law after being observed conducting séances by undercover female members of the Police Aid Detachment. Martha M'Clure was sentenced to a month in prison because there was evidence that M'Clure's 'inner circle' collected money to protect her from fines. She appealed against this judgement and the sentence was reduced to a fine. Nonetheless, the seriousness with which this matter was treated shows how the authorities were concerned about the effects of information from the other side of the grave.

Planchette-writing, table-turning and the like are often employed to relieve the tedium of winter evenings. Such practices do little harm to men and women whose minds are healthy; but there is a danger that through them persons, whose minds are unstable, may develop fixed illusions. Complete sanity is probably more rare than we imagine, and few have such mental stability that they can safely brood over one particular idea or for long concentrate attention on one particular mental state …

A tendency to mental instability is undoubtedly inherited. The weakness may be latent until a sudden emotional shock loosens the relation of thought to reality which we term sanity. Such shocks have latterly been numerous, owing to the war, and have led to a large increase in the number of individuals who firmly hold irrational beliefs. Among such beliefs, the idea that we can have constant communication with those whom we have loved and lost must be expected to show itself … I would remind those who think I have here made too unfavourable an estimate of a séance with the average medium that the law regards claims to spirit-intercourse as means whereby money is obtained under false pretences. Further, I would point out that the results of careful investigation of the characters and careers of celebrated mediums have usually been disquieting. Many of the ablest mediums of the past were proved to be dishonest. The more extravagant of their claims have now been generally abandoned. Half-a-century ago, a 'good' medium would commonly assert that his powers included materialisation of spirits, levitation and the like. Attempts to repeat apparently well-attested instances of such phenomena, under conditions sufficiently stringent to prevent the possibility of fraud failed. A cold critic will naturally suspect that the assertion of spirit-communication is similarly untrue, and that it continues to be made because credulous people are anxious to believe it and because, owing to its nature, disproof can hardly be conclusive.

Yet it would appear to be true that, associated with much deceit and with explanations that are false, successful mediums have genuine telepathic powers. They have thus been able to justify their claim to receive messages from the dead. I hold that such information is always obtained telepathically, that is, without physical means of communication, from the minds of the living. There are extremely few so-called proofs of spirit-intercourse that cannot be explained by the fact that the medium is reading the mind of the 'sitter.'[32]

The difference, if any, between Spiritualism and fortune-telling was under discussion at the Liverpool Police Court, yesterday, when a married woman named Martha M'Clure was charged on two informations with having pretended to tell fortunes (I) at the 'Christian Spiritualist

Church,' 60, Hope-street, on the 15th July, and (2) at her residence, 53, Erskine-street, on the 2nd August. The woman pleaded 'Not guilty.' She was defended by Mr Geddes.

For the prosecution chief Inspector Holbrook said that defendant held meetings at 60, Hope-street. Persons attending these meetings gave small sums of money. The police having received complaints of serious mischief having been caused by what the defendant told people, two ladies were sent to the place in Hope-street, as well as to her house in Erskine-street, where a kind of inner circle sat from time to time and where the same kind of thing went on.

Evidence for the prosecution was given by two lady members of the Police Aid Detachment ... On Sunday, July 15th, there were about twenty-eight persons present, all, with the exception of a man and a boy, being women. On the wall was a notice asking for a collection of 2*d* each. The meeting opened with a hymn, followed by a prayer, and during the singing of the hymn a collection was taken. Afterwards raffle tickets were sold, the proceeds for which, it was announced, would be sent to soldiers at the front. Later on, the congregation were asked to send up questions on paper. Mrs M'Clure answered eight of these questions. Every one of them dealt with the future. Witnesses sent up this question:

I should be glad to know if my husband is safe, as I have not heard from him for nine weeks. Will he come home safe?

The defendant answered, 'You will get news that your husband is safe. He is not in the firing line.' She added that she would like to see a letter from witnesses' husband. The answer to the second part of the question was, 'Yes, but not yet.'

Witnesses concocted a letter purporting to come from her husband, and took it to defendant's private house. Defendant handled the letter and said, 'I feel a pain in my left ear as though he is unconscious. He is alive, but he has had a bad time' ...

On leaving, witnesses asked defendant what she owed her, and she replied 'Nothing,' but witnesses insisted upon giving her a shilling ...

Mr Geddes said his client was a Spiritualist. She professes to be able to answer questions as a clairvoyant, not as a fortune-teller. She did not attempt to forecast the future, and she did not give the replies for monetary gain.

The defendant told the magistrate that she answered the questions to the best of her ability, through the aid of her 'spirit friends.' Of herself, she could not answer the questions. Out of the proceeds of the services at the hall many parcels had been sent to soldiers at the front. She did not accept any money for herself except what was subscribed by the inner circle at her house.

'I do not foretell the future. It is only the spirit friends that are with me that give me the messages, and I pass them on as I get them. I think it is a great comfort to these women to know something about the condition of their husbands or sons at the front.'[33]

The war against sexually transmitted diseases was stepped up during the First World War. As mentioned in Caldwell's report above, one of the functions of the female police officers was to move on and monitor prostitutes. By 1918, the army had followed the practice common in the navy and provided troops with a sanitising lotion that would be applied to the genitals after sexual intercourse. The value of such methods did not appear to impress T. W. N. Barlow, Wallasey's Medical Officer of Health. Maybe he felt that prophylaxis were not a reliable way to deal with the spread of the disease. Or perhaps Barlow thought that whatever their effectiveness, such methods would not reduce immorality.[34] Either way, Barlow was prepared to suggest quite radical methods to stamp out the 'social evil'. At the same time, however, he displays an awareness of the social stigma of venereal disease and recommended that there should be more privacy for those who are awaiting treatment.

Venereal diseases: Experiences in the defects of schemes with suggested reforms by T. W. N. Barlow MRCS, DPH Medical Officer of Health, Wallasey

Extract of paper read at Midland Branch, March 7th, 1918.

Dr T. W. N. Barlow opened the discussion by outlining the propaganda work carried out in the Liverpool area (which includes the four Country Boroughs of Liverpool, Bootle, Birkenhead, and Wallasey). This work is paid for by a joint contribution from the four municipalities in proportion to the population. Doubt was expressed as to the benefit likely to accrue from the propaganda work. Dr Barlow then gave figures showing the actual number of people who had come for treatment in the Venereal Diseases Centres in Wallasey (six months' working) and Bootle (nine months' working). There were two noticeable points in connection with both; one was the relatively small number of cases appearing for treatment; the second was the large number who had discontinued attending for treatment after one or two visits – about 75 per cent in both towns. He pointed out that this was a most serious state of affairs, and that unless remedied, it would result in the total failure of the objects of the schemes. In casting about for reasons for the non–continuance of attendance for treatment, it appeared to him that the congregation of people in one room waiting to see the doctor and incidentally opening up the possibility of meeting one of one's own friends, might be a reason for the disinclination to attend continuously. He suggested that in view of this that all treatment should be by appointment.

He did not agree with the mode of appointing the Venereal Diseases Officer, and pointed out that while municipalities now provided substantial sums out of the rates they had no voice whatever in the management of the schemes, consequently they were very disinclined to take any real interest in ensuring the success of the schemes.

Dr Barlow dealt with the question of prophylaxis and deprecated the forcing of this question to the forefront at the present time, while expressing the opinion that medical officers of health on being directly appealed to must explain the position so far as it is known in regard to the prevention of those diseases.

He then drew attention to recent legislation in New Zealand with regard to venereal disease, and concluded by expressing very strongly the opinion that *if we are to succeed in stamping out venereal disease*, we must have compulsory treatment and compulsory continuance of treatment until cured. As a first step in regard to notification he suggested that all cases coming for treatment should be told that if they discontinue the treatment until cured, the case would have to be notified to the medical officer of health. If this failed in having he desired effect, then there must be notification in every instance, accompanied by compulsory treatment until cured. The detention of people in prison found to be suffering from venereal disease until cured was also very desirable.[35]

There has been some debate over the motives of those who rioted after the sinking of the *Lusitania*. While some argue the disturbances were the result of xenophobia, others have called for more attention to be paid to economic hardship or emotional factors.[36] The importance of religion in Liverpool at this time is seen in the following extract. Although the paper concedes that the initial disturbances originated in Catholic areas, the greater outrages were perpetrated by Protestants. Despite the broad support for the war among Catholics and Protestants, 'Old labels persisted: the Liverpool Irish were still stigmatised as riotous and disloyal'.[37] Unfortunately, the *Lusitania* riots that took place from 8 to 11 May 1915 lent credence to these labels.

Once again, Liverpool is figuring in the eyes of the nation as a city of riots. Unfortunately, it is a position to which Liverpool has become sadly accustomed to occupying, for with the possible exception of Belfast, there is no great centre in the United Kingdom in which strenuous ebullitions of public feeling are more frequently witnessed, or more easily provoked.

Though there may never be justification for riots, they may sometimes be attended by extenuating circumstances, and most people who refuse to approve of the anti-German outbursts in which a section of the population has been indulging, are willing to admit that there may have been some extenuation for these, on the first day at least, and as far as a proportion of the participants were concerned. People, they say, and especially women of the poorer and less educated classes, who see their loved ones and their breadwinners, suddenly and without time to prepare snatched from them within sight of home, and hurled to death, cannot be expected to be too particular in the methods they select for ensuring that their indignation shall be fully appreciated by the available compatriots of the perpetrators of a dastardly outrage.

The relatives of a great number of the crew, both those who were lost and those who were saved, are residents of what is pre-eminently the Catholic portion of the city, and there have been efforts to make it seem that the riots originated with these people in their district. Such is not the fact. It is quite true that shops and houses in the Catholic quarter were wreaked and looted, and that some of the residents of the quarter took part in the work of destruction, but the Tory and anti-Catholic newspapers admit that the rioting began in Walton, the constituency of Mr F. E. Smith, and overflowed into Everton and Kirkdale, two other strongholds of Toryism and Orangeism, and that the most serious of Sunday night's outrages, the burning of a big confectionery factory, separated only by a narrow laneway from St Anthony's church and schools, was accomplished by a mob which swept down from the heights of Everton.[38]

4

Entertainment on the Home Front

Professional football was a controversial topic during the First World War. For one thing, sport's popularity was a problem. Yet its popularity became a problem when war broke out. As healthy young men, players were expected to serve. The same was true of many of the spectators. There was considerable criticism of the men who packed the football grounds and presented an alternative image to that of young men who abandoned civilian life and joined the colours. To see both going on at the same time disturbed the author of the letter below, and he was by no means alone. His comments and the supportive tone of the *Liverpool Courier* were replaying a long-standing argument about the place of professionalism in sport. There was also a divide between Rugby Union and Rugby League, as the latter version continued to play. Yet the majority of criticism was levelled at those who watched or dribbled the round ball.[1]

A gentleman holding high position in Liverpool's professional and commercial life desires us to publish the following:

To the editor of the Courier,

Sir, There must be two, no doubt accidental, omissions from the Football League's manifesto, published in the papers on the 1st inst. by Mr J. McKenna and Mr T. T. Charnley …

The first omission is that the manifesto does not in terms state, though it is surely to be implied from its patriotic language, that until the close of the war the players in League matches are to be men under 19 or over 35 years of age.

The second omission is that the manifesto does not in terms state that until the close of the war men between the age of 19 and 35 will only be admitted to watch League matches if they are wearing the King's uniform, unless, indeed, they produce at the gate a doctor's certificate ...

In this latter case the gatekeeper should be ready to supply the applicant with a card to be worn on the breast during the match, worded as follows:

'Not needed by my King and country.'

'Certified fit to watch League Football matches.'

Until I read the manifesto I had no idea that League Association football had such an exhilarating effect on spectators, and that these matches would stir up a patriotic spirit followed by a desire to serve the country. Much less did I appreciate what a cheery and comforting influence watching League matches is likely to have on the sad and those who 'sit and mourn,' especially in the days of sorrow now with us and yet to come.

I have never heard that doctors, ministers of religion, and other friends in their kindly efforts to alleviate the grief of the bereaved, have urged them to take a course of what might be termed 'football watching treatment.'

I am sure, however, that now that the suggestion has been so prominently brought forward by Messers McKenna and Charnley, the subject will be seriously considered.

I am surprised to note that so far no one has suggested that watching the kindred game of Rugby football is good for the mourner and the sad, but it is of interest to note that the exponents of Rugby football do not propose to continue their matches during the coming season. In fact, the leaders of the Rugby game, headed amongst others by Blackheath in the South and the Lancashire Rugby Union in the North, have unanimously come to the conclusion that it is not in the interests of the country that football should be encouraged during the coming season ...

Some persons with a turn for research may be able to enlighten the public as to why the attendance at professional and League Association matches is likely to advance patriotism and enlighten the hearts of mourners, but that the results do not ensue as compared with the attendance at Rugby and Amateur Association matches.

Yours,

An Old Public Schoolboy, Liverpool.[2]

As this summary of football on Merseyside at the start of the 1917-18 season shows, towards the end of war, football continued to entertain and draw crowds. Like other men who played sport, many footballers were eager to join the military. At the time team sports were seen as being akin to warfare. On paper, there was not much difference between the football field and the battlefield. Yet teams could still be fielded and games played, particularly in the north of England where those employed in protected trades took to the pitch on weekends without being accused of being unpatriotic. This report touches on the three foremost teams on Merseyside and displays a sense of regional pride in the performance of each team. A local man, Harry Lewis, is singled out for praise and he would continue to play for Liverpool until 1922 before joining Hull City.

There was a full programme of games billed for Saturday last, and the attendances were quite up to the average. To those who take little or no interest in the great winter pastime a big crowd at a football match during war time is somewhat puzzling, but it is simply their lack of interest which enables them not to see the enjoyment derived out of the sport by those who pay the piper. The quality of play was also quite up to expectations, although it must at once be admitted that such clubs as Everton, Liverpool, Tranmere Rovers, etc., have a distinct advantage over many of their rivals, this being due to the fact that they are within the area where a hive of industry gives them an opportunity of securing the services of many well-known exponents of the game who are engaged on munitions work. ...

To beat Bolton Wanderers by six clear goals, even at Anfield, is a feat which stamps Liverpool as a strong side, and, like their friends from across the park, they have yet to suffer the pangs of defeat, or, as a matter of fact, the loss of even one point. In their four contests up to Saturday last, the Reds have bagged eight points, with 16 goals against 2, a record which is only eclipsed by the 'Toffies.' On Saturday the

Anfielders were in great form, and the half-dozen goals were divided by Lewis and Bennett. The first-named is a youngster who hails from the North End of Birkenhead, and he is one of the best finds the Liverpool club has made since war broke out in 1914. Only Stoke can be added to the two Merseyside clubs as undefeated, but it will be of special interest to watch the result of next Saturday's games.[3]

This brief report of a match, between a female football team from a munitions factory and a team comprising soldiers, indicates how female footballers were treated as near equals. Women's football did not replace the male variety of the game during the war, but the opportunity to use FA grounds enabled some female teams to flourish.[4] The South Wales Borderers must have regretted giving the female players a two woman advantage. The Amatol Ladies hailed from Aintree and there was also an Amatol Management team. Aintree also had an Aintree Ladies Football Club. In January 1918, the *Liverpool Echo* mentions a charity match that was to take place between the Amatol Ladies and sailors from the Royal Navy in order to raise funds for the families of those who lost loved ones on HMS *Vanguard*. On that occasion the female team were not due to receive a handicap.[5]

Liverpool forward Harry Lewis.
(Author's collection)

The Amatol Ladies team visited Sniggery Camp on Saturday to play the return fixture with the Seaforth Garrison. The ladies were allowed the privilege of playing 13 members.

Final: Amatol Ladies 5, South Wales Borderers, 4.[6]

The following account demonstrates the lengths that were taken to keep football going on Merseyside during the war. After reinstituting a competition for juniors in 1916, the Liverpool Central Combination set up three leagues, although this was reduced to two in 1917–1918. With so many leading teams in the Lancashire section, there were plenty of players to inspire the juniors. Not only leading wartime players were worthy of admiration, however. There was the infamous game played on Good Friday of 1915, when Liverpool and Manchester United players who had placed bets on the result of the game orchestrated a 2–0 victory for United.[7] In 1917 the Liverpool outside left, Thomas Cunliffe, was suspended for 'indulging in coupon betting'.[8] These incidents should not take anything anyway from the football that was organised and played during the war, but they do show that it is difficult to idealise the sport. That said, perhaps the regulation that no players should be paid, enforced by the FA at the outset of the war, may well explain the occurrence of such incidents.

The Liverpool Central Combination caters for the footballer who is classed as a junior, and the committee are to be congratulated on having successfully carried on for another season.

For, in spite of the difficulties that were encountered, the Combination pulled through, being one of the few leagues who have contrived to keep the ball rolling during the war, and so provide the juniors with some recreation on Saturday afternoons.

One item worthy of special note is that the senior division has been able to find places for a large number of soldiers on leave, and also for discharged men who were still able to participate in the pastime.

The three divisions during the past season were made up of clubs from Liverpool, Birkenhead, Bootle, and Garston, and the honours were fairly evenly divided, as seven sets of medals were won by elevens on the Liverpool side and five by clubs across the water. Mersey and Orrell also qualified for cups, and Cammell Laird secured the other one.

During the last two months of the season several of the clubs were placed at a disadvantage owing to their grounds having to be taken over for the purposes of cultivation and they were consequently unable to complete their fixtures. The committee, however, express the hope that in the coming year the Parks and Gardens Committee will be able to see their way to throw open Stanley Park so that the boys can indulge in their favourite game.

The secretary wishes to apologise for the delay in calling the general meeting, and for the fact that the medals have not yet been presented, but this was unavoidable. The date of the meeting will be announced later and an invitation extended to elevens attached to munition works and certified trades to become members, but only clubs with grounds need apply. All particulars can be obtained from the league secretary, Mr T. Brown, 33, Brisbane-street, Kirkdale.[9]

Charity football matches were lively affairs and supplemented the regional league and junior games that also often included collections for charity. The following match had a nautical theme and brought the Merchant Navy up against the Royal Navy. Contemporary reports suggest that on this occasion 'Sailors' Week' was restricted to the northern part of Liverpool, where people could buy 'blue anchor' badges.[10] Reasons of national security probably prevented reference being made to the name of the Royal Navy's vessel. Charitable events like this football match were part of a week-long effort to raise money for the merchant navy. The presence of local notables at such events demonstrated the importance of the occasion: this was fun with a purpose.

Great interest was aroused in the football match which took place on Saturday, September 8th on the Waterloo Rugby Football ground between a team from S.S. *Metagama* and a team from one of His Majesty's Ships, in aid of 'Sailor's Week.' The proceedings were enlivened by music from the excellent band of the Boys' Refuge, St. Anne's-street, Liverpool. Much amusement was caused by Father Neptune in full regalia mounted on a piebald pony, who paraded the ground ...

The game started with an advance by *Metagama* on the right wing. After midfield play, Jackson received the ball, and passing to Wafer the latter scored a good goal. This reverse livened up the H.M.S. men, but the forwards were met by a splendid defence who were allowing no liberties. Still pressing, the Navy men were at last rewarded. Harkins after a tricky dribble passed to Marinsohn who showing a clean pair of heels to the defence and drawing Dobbs from his guard, scored with a broadside shot. Half-time arrived with the score 1–1. The Navy men kicked off in the second half. Splendid play by *Metagama* in which the whole forward line took part ended in Dingley giving a corner. This was well placed and kicked clear by McKenna. White received the ball from Neale and passing to Wheeler, the latter sent across to Marinshohn, who taking the ball on the run scored the second goal for H.M.S. *Metagama* had so far done most of the passing but seemed out of luck. A great shot by F. Robinson just tipped the bar. Edwards worked hard and was splendidly fed by Andrews. Full time arrived with the score – H.M.S., 2 goals; *Metagama*, 1 goal. The feature of the game was the great defence of both sides.

At the conclusion the football, which was given by Mr Jack Sharpe, the well-known sports outfitter of Liverpool, was sold by auction, and after keen bidding, it was knocked down to Miss Manning for 35s, who in a modest speech presented it to the captain of the team. The Chairman of the Council, Mr A. A. Lee, J.P., was an interested spectator of the whole of the game. The teams were afterwards entertained to tea. The Committee thank all those who helped to make the day such a great financial success.[11]

Horse racing, like football, attracted critics during the war. Not only was there the question of wasted horsepower, there were an array of arguments against continuing horse racing including the impression it gave to our allies. There were many who spoke out in favour of racing too, some of whom argued that football was far more wasteful than racing because it held back '22 sturdy men' from the army whereas racing employed small men, the majority of whom weighed under eight stone.[12] By May 1915, however, the government called on the stewards of the Jockey Club to halt all meetings with the exception of Newmarket, where all the classics took place during the war, on the grounds that use of trains to transport horses to race meetings would disrupt the haulage of war materiel. So, although the optimistic tone in the following report was vindicated, for the remainder of the war the Grand National was held at Gatwick racecourse.

Liverpool as a sporting city, regards at least one racing event per annum with intense interest. Some people who shun betting on any other phase of life's uncertainties make the Grand National the one exception to prove their rule. Hence a number of Liverpool folk are wondering whether the Grand National will be run this year. For the benefit of such it may be stated that it will take place in March as usual, unless very sensational and wholly unexpected war happenings occur. Racing 'over the sticks' is flourishing in a remarkable manner, being a trifle ahead of its former standard. At the outset of the season there was a possibility that the Grand National and all National Hunt sport would cease on account of there being an insufficient number of riders. The war, however, brought to England some French and Belgian jockeys, and now there is a mixture of nationalities in the weighing-room that is quite novel. Moreover, the plucky Belgians have had a good share of victories. There is every promise of a thrilling race at Aintree in March.[13]

Keeping pigeons during the war could be a costly pastime. Defence of the Realm regulations passed throughout the war prohibited or complicated many everyday activities. Although Liverpolitans were able to whistle for cabs (Londoners were forbidden to do this from April 1916), they faced a host of other restrictions. One of these involved getting a permit for keeping pigeons. If you were an 'enemy alien' you could not keep pigeons. Joseph Williams was one of many men fined for not registering their homing or carrier pigeons. Often, the accused would say they were unaware of the regulations. As for the pigeons, this was a time of relative safety. Defence of the Realm regulation 21A meant that anyone who shot a pigeon that did not belong to them could face up to six months in jail, a fine of £100, or both.

'These people who won't obey the law in these matters deserve to be punished.' Remarked the Stipendiary magistrate in fining Joseph Williams of Seagrave street 40s. and costs for keeping homing pigeons without a permit from the police.

Williams admitted the offence and said he had only bought the six homers at the weekend and had not had time to obtain a permit.

Mr H. Cripps, assistant police prosecutor, said from information received an officer called at defendant's house and found six homing pigeons upstairs in the top room and also between the ceiling and the roof. Next day he called and saw defendant, who said 'Oh, I bought two last Friday, two last Saturday, and two last Sunday, so that I had only had these birds for a very short time.'

He was told that other pigeons had been seen in his premises. He explained that those were some which he had had but had sold them. They had homed back to him, and he was keeping them for the owner.

The Stipendiary remarked that this was a serious offence. The Act of Parliament was passed for the protection of H.M. subjects, and it was expected that Englishmen would help the police to carry it out.

The defendant said he had to get the birds before he got the permit, but the Stipendiary retorted that he should have got the permit first.[14]

Baseball was a relatively rare sight in Britain, despite having been introduced to the island at the end of the nineteenth century. The presence of American and Canadian soldiers in the country, however, brought many Britons into contact with the sport, even if they were only introduced to the game when they read a newspaper report such as the one below. Relations between Britain and America had been improving from the late nineteenth century. Even so, American Independence Day (4 July) was not an anniversary that many Britons were aware of, let alone eager to celebrate. The arrival of American troops led to a greater awareness of all things American. An enemy had resulted in the tightening of existing common ties. Cultural exchanges, such as the baseball and football games at Port Sunlight, took place in towns where Americans were based or passed through.

At Port Sunlight on Saturday July 6th, as a sequel to American Independence Day celebrations, an exhibition baseball match was played on the football field by teams belonging to the American Army and Navy. The American Consul, Mr H. Lee Washington (and Mrs Washington) and a number of officers belonging to the Army and Navy of the United States, and other visitors were present, and were later in the day invited to take tea with the Hon, Mr and Mrs W. Hulme Lever at the Girls' Club. The officers, non-commissioned officers and men of the 'C' and 'D' Companies of the 2nd Battalion Cheshire Volunteer Regiment provided a tea for the teams, and about a hundred of their comrades in the Collegium. There was a great gathering of spectators at the baseball match, including wounded soldiers from Thornton Manor Hospital and elsewhere. Captain Lever, on the invitation of the teams, pitched the first ball, and the game was followed with the keenest interest, the clever pitching, the expert batting, and the quick returns of the ball evoking frequent applause, and much amusement being created by the mutual 'ragging' of the opposing teams, according to the well-known characteristic of a genuine bout of baseball. In the end the military team won, which was quite in accordance with the expectations of the sailors, who had naturally not the same opportunities for practice that are enjoyed by their comrades of the land service. After the baseball two of the Port Sunlight teams of lady footballers gave an exhibition of 'soccer,' which the American guests followed with the same keen appreciation as had been shown for their own performances. The American colours were in evidence throughout the village and in the entertaining halls during the day, and 'Old Glory' was, of course, particularly conspicuous on the football field.[15]

To help American soldiers feel a little more at home in Liverpool, the Round Table published a guide entitled *Places of interest and amusement for members of the naval and military forces of the Allies visiting Liverpool*. The list of places of interest, an assortment

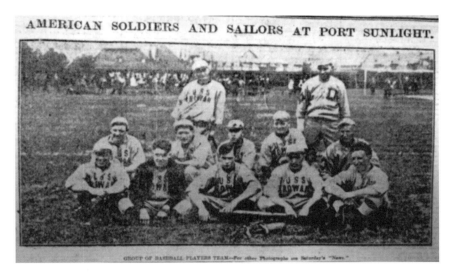

AMERICAN SOLDIERS AND SAILORS AT PORT SUNLIGHT.

American soldiers brought baseball to Merseyside. (Author's collection)

of facts, and a map of the city was accompanied by a welcome from the lord mayor and town clerk. Among other things, this guide demonstrates Liverpool's pride in and the desire of some notable figures in the port to entertain their American guests. There was concern among some Americans that their troops would be tempted by the seamier side of European ports.[16] This probably explains why the first arrivals at the Knotty Ash camp were not given passes to visit Liverpool. Yet, from the outset, officers visited the city on shopping trips for 'boots and trench coats'.[17]

Among the facilities highlighted by the guide were: St George's Hall; public libraries; Walker Art Gallery (featuring such morally uplifting works as W. Holman Hunt's *Triumph of the innocents* and G. Segantini's *The Punishment of Luxury*); the Lord Derby Museum of Natural History, which held 'An exhibition illustrative of Allotment cultivation and food production' in the great hall; the lord mayors' rest concerts for soldiers and sailors at St George's Hall on Sunday afternoons between 2 p.m. and 4 p.m., where 'smoking is allowed' and 'cigarettes are provided free during winter months'.

155

The harvest of the River is her revenue and she is the mart of nations.

Hospitality to American soldiers on leave. The Rotary clubs of the UK have undertaken and are now organising a scheme whereby American soldiers on Active Service who are introduced by American Rotarians or recommended by American Commanding Officers shall on obtaining leave be received as honoured guests in British and Irish homes.

Lord Mayor John Utting and Town Clerk E.R. Pickmere: 'Liverpool, the second city in England and the seaport of the greatest manufacturing district in the World, is often said to be the most American of all our cities. It is essentially a modern city, one of wonderfully rapid growth. The population in 1800 was 75,000. To-day it is over three-quarters of a million. The approximate total shipping of the port, inwards and outwards is 30 million tons a year. The port pays annually 7 million sterling in customs taxes. The municipal expenditure (1916) was £1,061,500. The municipal debt is 14 millions. Rents yield £549,484. The City Council invested one million sterling in War Loan Stock. The total area of the city is 26 sq miles.[18]

Entertainment was an important part of Edwardian life. The music halls had yet to lose their custom to cinemas, yet cinema was already a popular form of entertainment. Indeed, films were often part of the variety of entertainment provided at music hall venues. The following extracts tell us something about the role of cinema in Merseyside during the war. A request for cinemas to open on Christmas Day and show war films shows how patriotism and profit went hand in hand. The combination of war and religion might strike us as a little odd, but the main concern about Christmas showings was that the films 'were of a serious nature'. The increasing influence of cinema is seen in the second extract. According to the author of this letter, films about crime inspired juveniles to commit actual crimes. The question of what was behind the problem of juvenile crime was a regular topic for debate in the press during the war and cinema provided a convenient, visible answer.

The managers of thirty-six cinema theatres applied to Messrs W. W. Rutherford MP and A. G. Jeans at the Liverpool Police Court yesterday for permission to open their theatres on Christmas Day.

Mr Sanders (clerk) said that in the past years the cinema theatres had been opened on Christmas Day on the manager's undertaking that no comic films should be shown and that the films should depict scenes of an elevating character, as, for instance, scenery and travel.

Mr Rudd, who represented one theatre, asked the bench to sanction the display of war pictures. They were of a serious nature, and their exhibition might do good all round.

The bench agreed to the exhibition of war pictures, and sanctioned the opening of the theatres between 3pm and 10pm, on the understanding that all the managers were bound by the conditions laid down.

The chairman suggested that, inasmuch as the bench had made a concession in the matter of war pictures, the licensees might reciprocate by giving a proportion of their proceeds on Christmas Day to one or other of the war relief funds.

Mr Rudd said that he would refer the matter to his clients. He pointed out, however, that a very short time ago the Liverpool cinema proprietors gave the whole of their proceeds to war relief fund.

The Chairman: 'Yes, I know, but I thought some of you gentlemen would like to have the advertisement of doing a thing of this sort.'[19]

Sir, The increase in juvenile crime is at present causing great anxiety throughout the country. One of the reasons given for this serious state of affairs is the influence of a certain class of cinema films. Picturedromes undoubtedly attract children in a very remarkable manner, and it is, therefore, of the utmost importance that the pictures should be absolutely free from evil influence. It is, however, very much to be regretted that some films are proving very injurious to the young.

At a meeting of the Southport Town Council this week seven-day cinema licences were granted subject to the conditions that on Sunday, Good Friday, and Christmas Day no films should be shown depicting comedy or crime with serial films also being banned. Why should films depicting crime be allowed to appear on the screen at any time? Is it the opinion of the Southport Town council that films depicting crime cease to have any demoralising influence on the young when shown on any day but Sunday?

In a case at the London Sessions recently, in which two boys were bound over for breaking into flats and stealing goods to the value of £80, Sir R. Wallace KC, said: 'These picture palaces are the curse of London. This is proved by the multitude of cases which have come before me which have their origins in the pernicious influences of scenes and incidents depicted at cinema entertainments. In many of these places persons are represented in the act of committing crimes, suggesting to the youthful mind crime may be permitted.'

Surely the attention of the film censor should be drawn to this type of films. In addition to that children under sixteen years of age ought not to be allowed to enter picture palaces.

As the proper training of children is vital to the future well being of the nation, a great responsibility rests with parents and teachers with regard to their attitude in this matter. Apart from that it is also the duty of the State to take the necessary measures to protect the nation's children from the evil influence of certain cinema pictures.

Yours W. A. E.[20]

Theatre also provided excitement and education. In 1918 theatres across England were filled with people eager to see *Damaged Goods*. The following enticing description is not very explicit. What is meant by 'Damaged goods' and why is it for 'adults only'? Put simply, the play deals with play about venereal disease. It focuses on the consequences of a young man with syphilis who decides to marry, thus infecting not only his wife, but their baby and its wet nurse. The play had been censored in Paris, but was shown from 1905 and travelled to Broadway in 1913. By the time it reached St Helens in 1918, *Damaged Goods* had earned a reputation as a taboo-breaking play that was moral and educational.

Damaged Goods at Theatre. Next week's remarkable production.

A play for adults only.

On Monday next, June 10th, and during the week, there will be presented at the Theatre that wonderful and instructive play, 'Damaged

Goods,' a story of the hidden plague. It is the work of Eugene Brieux, member of the French Academy.

It contains no scene to provoke scandal or arouse disgust, nor is there in it any obscene word, and it may be witnessed by all, unless we are to believe that folly and ignorance are necessary conditions of female virtue.

These are the words addressed to the audience before the curtain goes up on 'Damaged Goods,' the great hidden plague play which has been and is still playing with such tremendous success at St Martin's Theatre London. The experience of these performances has proved beyond question that a play with a great moral purpose can attract and enchain the interest of a very large public.

The play teaches a terrible sermon, but it is such an [*sic*] one that has enthralled the people who have seen it with its tense dramatic moments, and its pitiless revelation of the cancerous growth that is gnawing at the heart of the civilised nations of the earth. The gallery at the St Martin's Theatre, as well as the stalls are always packed, showing therefore that all classes of people are represented. They are, in fact, wonderful audiences of both soldiers and civilians, and during the performance are hushed to silence by the grim intensity of this great human tragedy, therefore showing that the warning goes home.

Both women and men who see 'Damaged Goods' can never forget the lesson. No pulpit utterance could make the same tremendous appeal.[21]

Not all comedy and drama offered an 'escape' from the war. In fact, many plays and shows were popular because they addressed many issues raised by the conflict in a way that helped the audience come to terms with the consequences of war. This was certainly true of *Hullo! Baby*. Not only was the show set in wartime, some of the actors were discharged soldiers. After the introduction of conscription at the start of 1916, discharged soldiers provided a ready reserve of actors. In other papers the show, described as a musical farce, was touted as being 'up-to-date'. Although it was a light form of entertainment with catchy songs and jokes, many of the audience would have been aware that one of the actors had been gassed during the war. A play that visited Liverpool during the early months of the war is summarised in the following extract. *Sealed Orders*, an action-packed show full of espionage and conflict, helped allay fears of German airships and reassure audiences about the power of the Royal Navy.

The first visit to Bootle of the amusing and spectacular revue 'Hullo! Baby,' presented by Mr H. J. Snelson and Miss Queenie Craze, has been hailed with delight by the many Bootle playgoers who favour these productions. Though it cannot lay much claim to a plot, the artistes prove themselves very capable. Apart from the splendid acting all the male artistes deserve special support, as it is stated that they are either discharged soldiers or over military age. Another interesting fact is that the soldiers who appear in the hospital scene and the Victoria Station scene are all discharged soldiers who have fought overseas. The whole of the production is under the direction of Mr H. J. Snelson, and the music has been arranged by Mr Albert Vernon. The scenes are very complete and appropriately staged, the first represents Piccadilly Circus, the second a hospital ward in France, and the third the interior of Victoria Station, London. Throughout the play the audience are kept in a state of merriment by the amusing action and witty sayings of the artistes. Miss Queenie Craze, as Peg, is a huge success; and Mr Marmaduke Blobbs, who is well represented by Mr Ted Young is greatly in favour with the audience. Mr H. J. Snelson in the part of P.C. Buggins is very amusing and Mr Leonard Palmer proves himself a clever artiste as Charlie Blobbs. It is interesting to note that he has seen eleven months' service, and was severely wounded and gassed at Givenchy, La Bassée, before being discharged as totally unfit. Miss Dorothy Leamar as Baby Bunting, Miss Freda Elliott as Amelia Bunting, and Mr Archie McCraig as Tim Dexter, sustained their parts very cleverly, and the other artistes who comprise the thirty members of the company are thoroughly deserving of the vigorous applause which is accorded to them by the delighted audiences each evening.[22]

An appropriate booking has been made for next week at the Royal Court Theatre. 'Sealed Orders' is a warlike play, full of patriotic sentiments. In the story Britain is at war with a foreign country, whose people bear singularly German names. Interesting sidelights are thrown on international political intrigue and the secret service. It also demonstrates the use of aircraft and motorcars in times of stress, the importance of the Navy to England, and the advantage of big guns over airships. Excitement is enhanced by ingenious stage appliances. Among the scenes in which a melodramatic plot is enacted are a flower show, a gaming den, which is raided, a fight in space, a ball on the quarter-dock of a man-of-war, a race for freedom in motors, the wreaking of an airship, and a rescue from the sea. Mr Percy Hutchinson has rehearsed the company.[23]

Entertainment is a serious business. Tastes change and are influenced, and venues need to keep pace with these changes. Fortunately, Vesta Tilley got it wrong about the demise of pantomimes. However, the *Liverpool Echo* does concede that needed to invest in their pantomimes the Royal Court Theatre and the Hippodrome to ensure they were not eclipsed by revues. Reference is also made to the arrival of a song that would soon come to embody a spirit of resilience during the war. Before then, it seems, there had not been a standout war song. Finally, a few lines are spent on Madame Margo, who was called a 'mirthful mystic' who dispensed drinks to others, and appears to have had one too many. Seeing as one of her tricks involved the 'Glass Jug, which will give any drink called for', this mishap should come as no surprise. [24]

The pantomimes are nearing the end of their course, and with the sultry weather experiences in the last few days we have been inclined to say 'and high time, too, when summer is on us.' However, the panto season has had an almost unprecedented success, and Vesta Tilley's view that revues, with their gorgeous style and semi-pantomime ideas, will kill pantos, seems to be a shade wide of the target. At the end of December there was trembling regarding the panto shows. There was X., the unknown quantity, to be considered. However, well-built pantomimes were produced, and the enterprise of the management in spending money did the needful – namely, made money.

We heard someone a few days ago play one of the old rousing war-songs. The Boer war was a picnic to that obtaining now, yet no one has come forward with a real tearaway Tommy song. We have referred to this before, and would not have made further mention but for the fact that we recently paid tribute to the excellence of the song, 'Pack up your troubles in your old kit bag and smile,' and that tribute has been quoted by a theatrical paper, which adds this comment:

'It is interesting to note that, while all the winning songs in the recent 100 guinea song completion featured in these columns by Francis and Day, have more than justified their right to be included in the prize list, one of them has jumped right into the front rank of the year's song hits. This is the marching song, "Pack up your troubles in your old kit bag," and it is no exaggeration to say that. In the space of a few weeks only, it has won for itself a front place in the affections of the public. The chorus is conceived in the spirit of melodious optimism, and possess the infectious quality so essential in a song if it is to stand any change of becoming a great popular favourite...'

We saw an unusual scene this week at the Hippodrome, Liverpool. They had a packed house, and the no-treating order was being flagrantly defied. Mlle. Margo was generously calling for drinks, and she bore the expense. Half-way through her clever show she tripped on a step which had been placed in the stalls, and in a trice she had fainted. Fortunately her colour deceptions are now being carried on again, her ankle injury having healed nicely.[25]

There was always something exotic or funny on the stage. At the recently opened Garston Empire there were Charlie Chaplin films, comedic commentary on women's rights, acrobats and 'novelty instrumentalists'. Variety was about hitting the funny bone from every angle. The two entertainment reports below do not mention anything related to the war, although the audience would have been aware that the Hamamura Family were from Japan, an ally in the war against the Central Powers and the ventriloquist's 'topical patter' could have touched on the conflict. There were some critical comments, however, in the report about performers at the Liverpool Empire. Wartime audiences were not just passive consumers and tired of an oft-played tune or a worn-out joke.

The variety programme this week is again of a high order, pride of place being taken by the Sultan Bros., who give clever and quite original display as acrobats, and knockabout tumblers and dancers, introducing refreshing humour into their movements. Tom Franks provides a Ventriloquial entertainment with smart topical patter, and Linden and M'Grave are responsible for a burlesque on the eternal question of women's rights. In the pictures another Chaplin comedy heads the bill; for this week-end there are performances of 'Charlie's Night Out,' while throughout the next week 'Tilly's Punctured Romance,' a six-reel Chaplin, will be the great attraction. This picture is declared to be the greatest comedy ever produced, and the inimitable Charlie will be associated by Marie Dressler, Mabel Norman, and other popular Keystone favourites, in a film which provides 75 minutes' continual laughter. The star variety turns will be The Musical Keiths as novelty instrumentalists and operatic xylophonists, and Bert Groves, an eccentric comedian.[26]

Are not some of the leading music-hall stars sometimes in need of a reminder that they have visited Liverpool previous to 1916, and that people may visit a theatre more than once in a lifetime? A few of Wilkie Bard's numbers are certainly growing a little familiar to the music-hall patrons of the Mersey port. That is not to say that his artistry is not imprinted on them all still and of the same sterling quality, but it might find a new medium of expression. His reception from a well-attended house last evening was cordial. Whoever may be the song-writer for Morny Cash, that comedian might be well advised to stick to him. The material this artiste offers is not of a cheap order, and there is a distinct touch of simple individuality in its manner of presentation. Feats of acrobatic skill have this week some worthy exponents. The Hamamura Family of Japanese artistes are well to the fore in this department, and they reveal themselves as neat executants of somersault work. The Five Jovers are also clever acrobatic performers, and Manuel Vega presents an original individual trick act. A number strong in musical talent is given by the Denzilee Trio. A smart dancer is Cissie Lupino, while another smart terpsichorean artiste is the juvenile Doris Duquesne.[27]

We can almost imagine the laughter and expressions of the audiences in Liverpool and Birkenhead as they watched the following shows summarised below. The introduction of rationing at the start of 1918 was name-checked in the title of the Fred Karno revue. Karno was a force to be reckoned with in the entertainment industry. He was known as the man who set a young Charlie Chaplin 'on the right road'.[28] Robb Wilton was a Liverpool music hall artist who was known as the 'confidential comedian'. Performers like Wilton and 'son of Liverpool' Harry Angers gave music hall programmes a local flavour. The second report covers a range of performances, some of which sound like dramatised moral quandaries. Revd A. J. Waldron, the unconventional vicar from Brixton, believed that 'the variety stage was one of the best pulpits from which sex problems could be submitted to the judgement of the people'.[29] 'What would you do?' dealt with parents wondering how to react after their son's girlfriend had become pregnant.

There is a strong flavour of the topical about the programme at the Empire Theatre this week, since the title of the new Fred Karno revue presented is 'Rations!' It is not difficult to imagine that there are endless possibilities for amusement in a production with such a subject. Mr Robb Wilton and a fine company lose no opportunity of turning the good material to the most laughable account, with the result that the audiences are bound to enjoy the Karno 'Rations.' Prominent among the detached turns in the performance was Roxy La Rocca, the clever harpists, The Three Morellys, Dutch gymnasts, submit a thrilling act, and Sinclair's 'Three Diamonds' are sparkling singers and dancers.[30]

'The Gay Gordons' is to be the initial attraction of the autumn dramatic season at the New Theatre Royal, Birkenhead. This Seymour Hicks and Guy Jones piece is a bright and merry specimen of musical comedy. The Gordons are shown not at the front, fighting as they are now, but in their play hours. The hero of the story, Angus Graeme, is a private in the famous regiment. The company is headed by Mr Frank G. Dunn and Miss Empsie Bowman.

'A Soldier of the King' is the title of a new play which is to be produced for the first time in Liverpool next Monday evening at the Rotunda Theatre. The story, appropriately enough, deals with German intrigue, trickery, and spying. The author is Mr William Hibbert ...

What is described as a modern 'morality sensation' by the author of the much-discussed 'Should a Woman Tell?' the Rev. A. J. Waldron, is to be seen at the Empire on Monday. The new playlet, 'What Would You Do?' is to be submitted here for the first time on any stage. A capital verity bill supports it – the humorous studies of Ernest Shand; the joint efforts of John Terry and Miss Mabel Lambert in their series of caricature impersonations; Inez and Pim, comedy acrobats; George Benson, mimic; and the Four Holloways, who cycle upon swaying wires.

There will be a strong patriotic element in the coming programme at the Hippodrome. First on the bill are the Six Brothers Luck in 'Unsealed Orders,' a new comedy sketch, which will be played on Monday, Tuesday, and Wednesday. For the remainder of the week they are to produce for the first time 'Mad Dog,' a pantomimic sketch, which has for its subject the German Navy. There is also to be a novel rendering of 'Soldiers of the King,' with Mr Leslie Stuart conducting his popular work. The Annytos Trio of flying acrobats, a troupe of Belgians, who at the outbreak of the war were fulfilling a contract in Dresden; the Soho Trio of dancers and singers; Bi Bo Bi, in a bell act; and Miss Emily Hayes are also in the bill.[31]

What better way to assist the Belgian refugees than to eat Belgian chocolate? This novel idea was made all the more special by the addition of stardust in the form of performers from the world of entertainment, who would serve those who bought the chocolates. The event took place at Lewis's, one of Liverpool's premier department stores, and the money raised went to the *Daily Telegraph*'s Belgian Relief Fund. The author, Hall Caine, who appears in the extract about Port Sunlight's Horticultural show below, threw his support behind this campaign and published a book to raise money for the fund. This was a nationwide effort, and the presence of refugees throughout the country spurred on efforts

Music-hall star Wilkie Bard. (Author's collection)

to raise money for the displaced Belgians. Yet at the same time, the cause depended on local initiatives such as Liverpool's Belgian Chocolate Week that saw Lewis's decked out in the Belgian colours – black, yellow and red.

This week is to be known in Liverpool as Belgian Chocolate Week. Chocolates made by a famous Belgian firm are to be sold on behalf of the Belgian Refugees' Fund. But the novelty and additional charm of the scheme is that the chocolates will be sold by the leading stage celebrities at present appearing in Liverpool Pantomime, and these popular favourites will sign their names upon each box of sweetmeats which pass through their hands. The facilities for conducting the sale have been kindly provided by Lewis's of Ranelagh-street, whose attractively decorated sweet department has been placed at the disposal of these charming and talented artistes, ever ready to come forward and help the cause of charity.

The public will doubtless rise to the occasion and avail themselves of a scheme that offers a three-fold pleasure. In the first instance there is a box of delicious chocolates to be received from the hands of a stage artiste; that box will bear the autograph of the lady or gentleman in question; and a portion of the money paid for the chocolate will be handed over to the 'Daily Telegraph' Belgian Relief Fund. Thus one may have the satisfaction of obtaining the autograph of your favourite actor or actress on a lovely box of chocolates, at the same time materially benefiting the Belgian Relief Fund. It is a proposition that must instantly appeal to Liverpool citizens in one or more of its various aspects.

Lewis's, therefore, will during Chocolate Week become an even more favoured resort than ever. It is obvious, of course, in view of the heavy and responsible duties which the ladies and gentlemen have to perform in connection with pantomime that there must be a limitation to the hours at which they can undertake to play the role of saleswomen and salesmen on behalf of charity. By common consent the hours for chocolate sales have been fixed at from noon to 4.30pm. The public can thus make their arrangements accordingly ...

With such charm and talent in charge of the sweet department, it is difficult to conceive how anyone can resist the temptation to pay a visit and buy a Belgian box of chocolate. The prices have been fixed to suit every purse – 5s, 3s, and 1s 6d per box – so that everybody will be able to assist the object for which all this preparation and effort is being made.

This scheme possesses many attractions which do not appear on the surface. For instance, we can readily imagine that the talented sellers of these confections will have some original methods of disposing of their wares ... Many a merry jest will doubtless pass across the counter between the seller and the purchaser ... Is there a Liverpolitan who can miss this opportunity?[32]

At horticultural shows, nature took centre stage. Those on the home front knew about the effect of artillery on the landscape of France and Belgium: shattered buildings, fields laid waste, and forests reduced to blackened tree trunks. The work of farmers, foresters and builders were undone by war. That is not to say that the show was untouched by the war. For instance, the demands of the war meant that flowers were not as common as vegetables. Yet the occasion enabled a very distinctive community based on the philanthropic vision of William Lever to note the importance of flowers. The novelist Hall Caine provided touching evocation of the power of flowers at the side of a wounded soldier's bed. Caine stopped writing novels after the war broke out and offered his literary services to the government by writing war reports that were relayed to allied counties.

Port Sunlight Horticultural Society held its 23rd annual show in the Auditorium, Port Sunlight, on Saturday, and although the entries were not so numerous as last year all the classes were well represented and formed a very attractive and encouraging display, enhanced by the admirable arrangements ...

In opening the proceedings Lord Leverhulme said it was his duty to welcome Mr Hall Caine to their presence, and they felt greatly honoured in having him with them, not only because of his outstanding place in English literature, but in addition because of his human sympathy with the workers in the United Kingdom. That sympathy was shown in his writings and by his active work on their behalf. They were looking forward that afternoon to showing him what Port Sunlight was like. That show was one of Port Sunlight's institutions, and one to which they were justly proud. They were particularly proud that year because they were seeing the effect of war work. He was told by the secretary that flowers had largely given way to vegetables, and a record had been attained in production ... Much of the work had been done by the women, and the spirit of the women of England was typified by the reply made by one at Bromborough that she wished they would let them go out to the Front, in response to a comment by him (Lord Leverhulme) that they were proud of them and that they were doing just as much to help win the war by their work at home. They were greatly honoured to have with them also that day, on her first visit to Port Sunlight, Miss Olga Nethersole, who was greatly interested in the work the ladies were doing ...

Caine: 'There is something very human in flowers. A great writer (I am afraid he was a German) said he once fancied a paradise for the spirits of departed flowers. When they die they go, he said, not to heaven or to hell, but to a middle state, a kind of blessed purgatory. The souls of the lilies enter into young maids' foreheads; those of hyacinths and forget-me-nots go into their eyes, and those of irises into their lips. However this may be (and being a man I am, of course, bound to believe it), I know that flowers speak very closely to the human heart at certain shadowed moments of life. It is not for nothing that we fill the sickroom with flowers. In doing so we are answering some mysterious and unspoken call of the human soul for the joy and inspiration of returning health. Flowers need no language save their beauty to convey their message. Going through some of the military hospitals which the war has scattered through the country, I have seen the delight that the wounded soldiers get out of the flowers, which good people send them. Rough fellows, many of them, straight out of the mud and filth and slime of the trenches, yet taking joy in the little pots of lilies and roses on the shelves by their bedsides.'[33]

In 1917, the Welsh National Eisteddfod was held in Birkenhead. It provided an opportunity for both entertainment and commemoration. The purpose of the eisteddfod was to uplift the Welsh nation and maintain poetic and musical tradition. Although very different to the kind of performances that would be heard in music halls, the eisteddfod was still a place of entertainment, albeit edifying rather than exciting. The absence of the prizewinner, Ellis Humphrey Evans, who used the bardic name *Hedd Wyn*, was marked by the chair that he would have sat upon to be crowned bard being draped in black. Evans, who served with the Royal Welsh Fusiliers, had been killed at Pilckem Ridge in 1917. Lloyd George attended the eisteddfod and declared that such events calmed the spirit and reminded all of the importance of national unity and how the British Empire contained many proud and distinct peoples, including the Welsh.

No more remarkable series of incidents has occurred at any Eisteddfod during the last thirty years as those which marked the closing session of the Eisteddfod of 1917, which consequently will be memorable for generations to come. The appearance on the platform in the morning of the sole survivor crippled for life, of a choir of Welsh Fusiliers which won a prize at the Bangor Eisteddfod of 1915, and shortly went to France and were destroyed, was poignantly pathetic. Following this in the afternoon session came the stunning episode of the dead shepherd-poet, the winner of the chair prize, who when his victory came to be announced had been 'lying in his silent grave in a foreign land' since July. The empty chair was draped with symbols of mourning, and the 'Black Chair of Birkenhead' will go down in history along with that of Wrexham of some thirty-five years ago. Llew Tegid's handling of the first incident was a triumph; that of the second by Dyfed and his bards was an even more impressive dramatic demonstration, fitly rounded off by noble elegiac stanzas. Finally, the presence at the afternoon session of the Premier and his uplifting speech was a third outstanding feature of a successful and historic festival.[34]

German bands were a common sight and sound in Britain during the late Victorian and Edwardian periods. However, even before the war they were not always welcome. Some disliked the noise, others the nationality of the musicians. With the outbreak of war, though, even those who had enjoyed the music and not given much thought to the nationality of the band members began to reassess their local German musicians. The fates of these bands were fairly similar as they faded from the streets, bandstands and charity events. Usually, it is difficult to trace the exact nature of their demise on the local level. This report from Wirral offers some useful details about the fortunes of what was called West Kirby's 'Town Band'.

National feeling ran high at West Kirby on Wednesday when, according to a report from the district, a number of Deesiders entered into a hostile demonstration against the Town Band. The band consisted of about a dozen Bavarians, the majority of whom have lived in Hoylake or West Kirby for a number of years. The conductor and proprietor, Herr Groop, has made himself very popular in the district, largely on account of his ever-readiness to place his band at the disposal of the organisers of any charitable project.

It is understood that after the usual calls had been paid, and the usual coppers collected, the band, in a moment of uncontrollable patriotic fervour struck up 'Der Wacht am Rhine.' This appears to have been too much for those who heard the strains and one of those near went up to Herr Groop and asked him to change his tune. So far as can be gathered, Herr Groop did not object to changing his tune so long as he was left at liberty to strike up whatever he liked. This was objected to, and from a score of British throats came the demand that he should strike up 'Rule Britannia' and put all the energy and feeling he had into it, and also that the brass should resound with all the force of then combined cubic capacity of the lungs of his assistants. This was too much. 'No "Rule Brittania," no tune at all' was the watchword of the Britishers in the vicinity, and Herr Groop at length found himself compelled to make a hasty instrumental retreat.

It is reported that the band subsequently came to the conclusion that there was 'no place like home' and left the district the following day to the strains of that pathetic little ballad.[35]

Getting to know, and understand, the opposite sex often took place during dances. This was particularly true for 'B', the author of an article that gives us an idea of what one, educated young man thought about men, women, fashion and the changing times. He called for men to take on board more colour in their wardrobe. Not all men restricted themselves to black, but 'B' does have a point. In general, men were far from being peacocks and maybe this sense of all men being alike was heightened by the uniforms worn during the war. There was another reason for his interest in colour, however. He wanted to communicate with the ladies he met at dances, to bridge the gap between the sexes. The call, at the end of his article, to break free from old habits is something that many others shared at a time when the end of the war was in sight.

A Colour-scheme for men

Being one of six sisterless sons, I know but little of the wiles of womankind, my knowledge being gleaned solely from attendance at various dances (where men see more of girls than anywhere else).

There I see the pallid girl, decked in pink, shewing the beauty of her white neck; and there the red-haired girl, clad all in white, gives me a reason for the continuance of certain dyes made for those who envy, but can never possess, such tresses.

This only serves to make me sad. Man must be ever clothed in black. No man may differ by so much as a tie, from his friends, or any waiters present. Surely suits of such dull shades as brown, maroon or bottle-green would still shew girls' frocks to advantage, and what I want to impress is the fact that it would benefit the men to have some choice.

This variety would enable a man to be found by his partner, and secondly to entertain her better while 'sitting out.' As it is, the mere mention of 'dresses of the evening' from my partner, forces me to use my stopper in the form of 'Last Saturday at football ...'

'Experience teaches,' and I have never repeated the folly of my first dance. On that occasion a siren mentioned the sweet frock of a passing girl. I (poor fool!), appeared interested, and said I preferred pink to blue; and thought satin was nicer than silk.

My fate was sealed: my nymph plunged into a series of zoological epithets amongst which I faintly caught 'elephant-grey' and 'peacock-blue.'

I smiled weakly, and expressed an admiration for 'robin-red.'

My partner did not appear to notice my remark but continued to speak in Greek. I caught such awful words as 'crêpe-de-Chine' and 'Axminster,' and some even worse expressions.

When she stopped for breath, I pointed out the dress I most admired, which I described as being pink satin. To my consternation I was informed that in future I must know this material to be Argenta Taffeta.

I felt that I was beaten: with a sickly smile I led her down to supper, hoping to fill her mouth with jelly or fruit-salad.

As well attempt to check Niagara with a brick! She prattled gaily on, presenting me with large supplies of blanc-mange; and finally left me in a demoralised condition, feeling as never before, that I was but a mere man.

Another type of girl we meet is she who blushingly returns one's programme marked like this – 'H.L.' What is to be done to this type of girl? Why is she annoyed because we cannot find her later?

With a more intimate knowledge of colours we men might readily note their dresses upon our card. As it does, not knowing one shade of mauve from another, I am forced to put in the minute available space some personal description of my partners. My old programmes contain such gems as 'Pink and Powdered,' 'Pearls and Plain,' 'Sweet and Low,' *cum multis aliis* [with many others].

The possible effect of the damsels discovering one of my cards causes me many a sleepless might.

Therefore, with all diffidence, I venture to suggest that men should throw off the yoke laid upon them by their fore-parents, and revel in the joys of choice twixt 'nigger,' 'navy' and 'maroon.'

B.[36]

Wartime on the home front was broken up by series of special 'flag' days when money would be raised for specific war-related causes. With so many allies and organisations to support, these flag-day events were a regular occurrence. Indeed, the forthright requests for donations upset some people who felt they were being pestered rather than invited to contribute. Yet flag days such as the one in Crosby, described in the first source below, were beneficial not only because money was raised for needy allies or organisations, but also because it helped solidify relationships between the allies, help people on the home front feel part of the war effort and provided plenty of entertainment and colour. Some places maintained their traditional celebrations. As the second extract shows, this provided a glimpse of pre-war and post-war, times that stirred memories and helped lift the spirits of Bootle's residents almost three years into the war. Even so, such celebrations were of less duration than their equivalents. Or, as in the case of Bootle's 'May Day', they were not celebrated at their usual point in the calendar. On occasions when demands were placed on workers to maximise output, there were calls for traditional holidays to be cancelled or postponed. The third extract, from *St Helens Newspaper*, indicates how the government decision to postpone the Whitsuntide holiday was not taken lightly. Concessions needed to be made for the war effort, but at the same time there was recognition of the importance of leisure and recreation.

In response to a communication which has been received by Councillor T. C. Walker, J.P., chairman of the Litherland Council, arrangements are being made to observe in a suitable way France's National Day in the Litherland district. We believe Mr Walker is in communication with the head teachers of all the schools and he has requested them to give short addresses to the children on July 12th, in order to impress upon their minds the national anniversary of our great Ally. France's National Day, July 14th, falls on Sunday this year, and it is suggested that it should be celebrated in this country on the 12th. Mr Walker hopes to make further arrangements so as to celebrate the anniversary in accordance with the request he has received. He would be glad if residents and proprietors of works would kindly, as far as possible, exhibit French flags on the 12th inst. An observance of the French National Day would be a graceful compliment to the nation, especially as the French Mayors and civic authorities took an active part in the celebration of St. George's Day, and demonstrations and meetings were held in all the leading cities of France. The celebration will include a message from the Council expressing to the President of the French Republic the goodwill of the residents, and it is hoped that the Marseillaise will be played at all entertainments. It is proposed to compile an official list of all the cities and towns in this county where the French National Day is celebrated and it will be presented to the French President. The French anniversary was also considered at the meeting of the Great Crosby Council on Wednesday evening, and the arrangements for the celebration of the Crosby district were left in the hands of the chairman, who promised that he would give the matter his earnest consideration.[37]

Saturday was almost like old times – it brought back a sweetly scented breath from the days when peace and plenty were our portion and when our only trouble was the discordance of the political market-place, where from different booths different showmen entreated us to believe that Codlin was the friend, not Short, in some fly bitten controversy that seems curiously distant to-day.

But with Saturday came memoires of Bootle's own especial three day's carnival – the May Day Fete. True, it was only a one-day show, and that swing boats and roundabouts, ice cream and shooting galleries, blazing lights and shrill brass music, found no place in the programme. Yet it was remarkably like the real article (as Sam Weller observed of the special constables baton), in several ways. There was a procession – there was a collection along the route – and the aim of it all was to give a helping hand to Bootle's foremost charitable institution. In short, it was the Flower Day and Motor Procession which at the request of the Mayor of the Borough the Bootle May Day Committee had organised to help the funds of the Borough Hospital. Before the war the income of this admirable institution was swelled yearly by sums ranging from £500 to £600 as the fruit of the May Day Committee's activities, but since the outbreak of war the annual carnival has been in abeyance and the funds have suffered in proportion, although the demands upon the hospital have increased ...

The main feature of the programme viewed through financial spectacles, was the sale of flowers in the streets, but from the spectacular view-point the attraction was the motor procession through Bootle, Litherland, Seaforth, and Waterloo – though even here business was business, and a street collection was vigorously pursued by charmingly dressed young ladies, many of whom had only a short time before [they] doffed the khaki overalls of the munition worker ...

An immense crowd had gathered at the Town Hall to see the procession start, and the wait was enlivened by selections played by the Bootle Municipal Band under the conductorship of Mr Workman (bandmaster).

The motor fire-engine of the Bootle Fire Brigade, which with its gleaming brass-work and brilliant vermillion partially hidden under delicately tinted festoons of flowers made a striking feature, was in the forefront of the procession, manned by a detachment of the Brigade under Supt. J. Cole; the horse-ambulance tastefully hung with flowers, the horse-engine with the Unicorn team of horses; the Corporation motor-car; the Municipal Military Band, in a steam-wagon and trailer lent by Messrs. Rowe Bros. and Co. Ltd; and the engine and a detachment of members of the Waterloo-with-Seaforth Fire Brigade …

The flower selected for the day was the Parma violet and so successful were the lady sellers that the supply ran short during the day. A number of ladies came to the rescue, and spent many hours making a further supply, and by the evening it would have been easier to find the proverbial needle in the proverbial haystack than a man, woman, or child who was not wearing the delicately coloured bloom. Everyone was doing it – soldiers, sailors, policemen, aldermen, councillors, magistrates, ladies in moussclaine, ladies in shawls, and all the intermediate grades between – shall we say – Oxford-road and Miller's Bridge.[38]

The appeal to munitions workers to forgo or shorten their holiday at Whitsuntide is evidence that the supply of shells and guns is not too ample for the needs of the Army. Mr Lloyd George's anxiety to prevent any diminution of output suggests, indeed, that there might easily be a shortage if anything like a general engagement all along the British line were to take place just now. Seeing that there has not been even a start of the 'great advance' which had been predicted for the early summer, we had been led to believe that the tremendous reserves of shells which have been accumulating for months were sufficient for any emergency. This is evidently not the fact. We are being told very plainly that any reduction in the production of shells and guns means a corresponding increase in the casualties of our soldiers. There is no reason for doubting the honesty and urgency of the appeal to the men who are helping to win the war in the munition factories and in the coal mines. And there can be only one response to the appeal. The loyalty and patriotism of munition men and miners were demonstrated by the willing sacrifice of the days of rest and recuperation to which they look forward at Whitsuntide. There is really no alternative for men who realise that the lives of their brothers in the trenches are dependent on their maintenance of the output of shells and guns. The tremendous daily expenditure of shells by the Germans shows that our enemies, in spite of our blockade, are still able to feed their guns without stint, and it is of the highest importance that our artillery should be in a position to deluge the German lines with fire whenever and wherever it becomes necessary. Some of the Miners' Associations have already taken the lead and are advising their members to limit the Whit-week stoppage to one day, and there is every reason to hope that that policy will be generally adopted by the miners. As regards the actual makers of shells and guns it is anticipated that there will be a postponement of the Whitsuntide holidays until August 8th. Mr Lloyd George appealed to the Labour Committee on War Output on Monday, to prevent any diminution in the output of essential military supplies by postponing the holidays for two months. He declared that such action would save thousands of lives. The delegates were assured by Mr Henderson that the Government would compensate those workers who suffered pecuniary loss through having made their holiday arrangements. It was also suggested that, if necessary, the decision would be backed by legislation. The Mayor Alderman Bates has expressed his approval and makes what is practically an appeal to all workers to 'carry on' until the extended August holiday.[39]

New Brighton, August Bank Holiday 1917. (Author's collection)

5

Remembering, Celebrating and Commemorating

Today we are used to seeing imposing war memorials in almost every village and town. It is, therefore, easy to overlook the fact that there were other ways of commemorating those who had died in war. The monuments and plaques erected after the war were the culmination of a long process of collective, public mourning. Often the first public act of honouring the dead would be a report, and possibly a photograph, in the local press. Mourning on a personal or family level would take the form of a photograph or other item that reminded them of the deceased relative. Some workplaces or places of worship would have their own ways of remembering those who served, and the dead. One of the most striking community-based means of remembering the fallen was the street shrine. First recorded in Hackney during the summer of 1915, street shrines are believed to 'be a form of commemoration particular to London'.[1] This letter to the *Wallasey News* published during the summer of 1917 indicates otherwise.

Sir,

Last night (Sunday) I made my way down to Silverlea-avenue to see the unveiling of the first war shrine in the North of England; as from the conflicting rumours one heard about it, I was anxious to see for myself if all one heard was true.

The shrine takes the form of a wooden tablet secured to the wall of one of the houses, and contains printed upon white paper under a glass covering the names of a large number of those, presumably in connection with St. Mary's parish, who have fought and died in this great war.

There can be no objection to such a list of worthies; we all would honour those who have given their lives – heroes as they all are – for such a noble cause – the fight for freedom. But herein is the inconsistency, that whilst honouring the champions of freedom there are features, I am grieved to say, about this particular shrine which must have an influence, not on the side of freedom, but the reverse. The Romish crosses and the quotation from Thessalonians at the bottom of the shrine are intended to lead the unwary from the faith once delivered to the saints.

The quotation reads as under:

'We give thanks to God always for you all, making mention of you in our prayers.'

What can the meaning of this be, if not intended to give sanction and authority to prayers for the dead?

I know not who is responsible for the shrine, but I say, whoever it is, he cannot call himself an honest man. He must surely know that St. Paul was not addressing the dead in his epistle, but the living Church, and yet taking a mean advantage of ill-educated people, using the quotation for an unlawful purpose. St. Paul never prayed for the dead.

Yours, etc., Renton Gibbs.[2]

Memorials did not just spring up overnight. Committees deliberated about the monument's design, size, location and cost. These memorials would represent the men who died and those who fought, so it was important that the final decisions were as agreeable to as many people as possible, especially those who had lost loved ones in the war. There were discussions about what was the most appropriate way to remember the dead. All may have agreed about the need for some type of memorial, but there were disagreements about what form the memorial should take: some preferred memorials that would serve a social function, others favoured monuments. Although politics did play a part in debates, there was no clear-cut divide over which party or ideology favoured a particular form of commemoration.[3] In the case below, the 'Vicar's letter' in the Dunstan parish paper shows that spatial and aesthetic matters played an important part in the deliberations about where to place a memorial.

My Dear Friends,

Our memorial is making good progress. Up to the present, we have received promises and cash to the value of £200, and I have no doubt that we shall, ere long, have received all that we require.

The Committee has decided to make certain alterations which, in the opinion of all the members, are improvements. A very handsome Celtic cross has been obtained, which our architect will mount on a suitable pedestal, of sufficient size to allow all the names of the fallen to be engraved upon it. We have also decided to change the position of the cross. Originally, it was intended to place it beneath the west window of the Church; but, I must confess that none of us were very happy about it, as we felt that it would be so very much overshadowed by the Church, and, at the same time, suffer from the very confined space between the Church and the surrounding wall. Happily, a thought came into our minds, upon which we have determined to act. We propose to remove a large portion of the wall on the Earle Road side of the Vicarage garden and replace it by railings, behind which the cross will be placed. It will be completely railed round, and shrubs will be planted behind it. There will be a gate in Earle Road, so that any who wish can enter the enclosure for the purpose of placing flowers. We believe that this position will show off the beauty of the Memorial which will be very conspicuous. I trust that those who desire the names of their dear ones to be engraved will send them as soon as possible, and that those who desire to contribute will give their names to the Wardens at once.

Believe me,

Your affectionate priest and friend

W. O. Hunter Rodwell.[4]

Memorials are intended to represent not only the dead but the mourners and the population of the area as a whole. This is not always easy to achieve. In the case of St Dunstan's Parish, the memorial could represent members of a particular denomination.

When it came to a city-wide memorial, however, it was important that all groups were represented and were satisfied with the location of the memorial. A report from a local paper towards the end of 1917 stresses the representative nature of the £50,000 memorial that was being planned for the Anglican Cathedral. In a city with a large Catholic population, as well as other Protestant denominations and faiths, it was vital that the proposed memorial did not represent any particular denomination. Nonetheless, it is unlikely that all residents of the port would have agreed with the claim that the yet to be completed cathedral was 'the supreme symbol of the city's Christianity'.

It is a worthy and fortunate inspiration that one of the transepts of the Liverpool Cathedral should be erected in memory of the soldiers and sailors of the Liverpool diocese who have given their lives in the cause of righteousness between the nations. Just as there could be no nobler sacrifice than they have made, so there could be no nobler memorial of their glory and their death than that which is now proposed.

The suggestion has been made as a result of a spontaneous and widespread impulse that gives it an especial significance. The movement was initiated by very representative and influential citizens who hold different creeds, belong to different parties, and are engaged in different forms of business activity but who are all united in the belief that it is by this splendid addition to the city's great testimony in stone of its living faith that we can most fittingly and most reverently commemorate the heroic deed.

The Cathedral is an emblem of the faith in which our nation has gone to battle. Had there existed no such spirit in England as that in which this gift to God is being prepared, there would have been none of the Christian Chivalry which made our people unhesitatingly take their stand ... when all the world was asking what Britain would do. The spirit is not denominational, but national; it is a nobleness created by the teaching of all Christian bodies. And because the Cathedral is the supreme symbol of the city's Christianity it is most fitting that in the building itself should be embodied the city's gratitude to those who have

LIVERPOOL CATHEDRAL, WAR MEMORIAL TRANSEPT.

The Anglican cathedral war memorial. (Author's collection)

fought and fallen in the name of the ideals to which the great church itself is reared.[5]

This report from the *Birkenhead News* presents an example of a utilitarian memorial. Such practical memorials were, however, relatively rare. Of all the war memorials in the British Isles, less than 10 per cent served a practical purpose, such as hospitals, parks or village halls.[6] The hospital ward at Birkenhead was in memory of one man, yet would help many other people. Not everyone could afford such acts of charity. Even in this case, the local council paid for the ward to be equipped. As meat traders, the Robinson family would have witnessed some turbulent scenes in Birkenhead at the start of 1918. Despite being a hub for the cattle trade, Birkenhead reduced its meat ration to ½ lb per person on 4 February 1918, compared with 1 lb in Wallasey.

On Tuesday afternoon Birkenhead's Mayor (Alderman M. Byrne) formally opened at the Borough Hospital the 'James Robinson' Memorial Ward, which has been provided by salesmen at the Woodside Lairagee by retail meat traders in the borough and district, and by Mr R. J. Robinson (father) to the memory of the late Second-Lieut. J. Robinson, 9th K.L.R., who met with his death in France in May of last year.

The inscription on the marble tablet at the entrance to the ward runs as follows: 'This ward has been endowed in memory of Second-Lieut. J. Robinson, 9th K.L.R., who was killed in France, May 29th 1917, as a tribute and memorial of a beautiful, heroic, and unselfish life, by his many friends and his proud and devoted father.'

The ward in question, it may be mentioned, adjoins that in which at present is placed the bust of the martyred Nurse Cavell ...

The Mayor, in opening the proceedings, testified to the high esteem in which the family of Mr R. J. Robinson had always been held in Birkenhead. He himself had known four generations of them, Mr Robinson, his father, his son who had fallen, and grand-children of Mr R. J. Robinson. He thought Mr Weightman and his colleagues associated with the hospital, and the other hospitals in the town – the Children's

Hospital and the Maternity Hospital – would find that now the meat trade was taking an interest in their institutions they would get a very substantial sum of money yearly to help them through their difficulties. He (Alderman Byrne) said without fear of contradiction that there was no body of traders more open-hearted or more generous to help those who were down or in distress than the meat traders. They had met that day to show their respect for the memory of one who was respected by everyone that knew him. They were showing that respect in a tangible form, in a form that would keep green forever the memory of Lieut. James Robinson. Generations that came after them would have in the 'James Robinson' Ward a memento of the great war in which one of Birkenhead's gallant sons fought and gave his bright and promising young life for his country. That day would, he believed, mark a new era in the work of their trade so far as regarded their conception of the duties which devolved upon them as citizens. He thought that as a trade the meat dealers ought to be more represented upon the public bodies, and he suggested they should take steps to that end. The Mayor then proceeded to present to Mr Weightman a cheque for £1,000 for the endowment of the Memorial Ward. He understood that was the first time in the history of the hospital, since it was built by the Laird family, that a full ward had been endowed by members of one trade in this manner. He hoped, however, that the example set that day would be followed by other trades. But it was no use having a ward without equipment – especially when they knew that they had at present an epidemic raging around them which was giving Birkenhead, unfortunately, one of the highest death rates in England. Therefore he had also to hand over a cheque for £114 5s to Mr Weightman for the equipment of the Memorial Ward.[7]

During a debate about the Imperial War Graves Commission in the House of Commons in December 1919, Major Benn Jack Brunel Cohen, MP for Liverpool Fairfield, gave his opinion about the most appropriate gravestones for the fallen. Some MPs thought it was quite unfair to suggest that all stones should be alike in the cemeteries on the continent. The families ought to be able to select and purchase whichever stone they wished. Cohen, on the other hand, argued that all stones should be identical. While some others thought this stance put the interests of bureaucracy over the feelings of family members and individual choice, Cohen saw war as a great leveller. He had lost both legs below the knee to the war, and a brother.

Major Cohen: I want to throw any little weight I have on the side of the Hon. Member who has just spoken. My desire is to give the point of view of a man who has been out there and the point of view of the men who lie there now. We did not think very much about death when we were out there, but we did think a great deal of comradeship, and I cannot imagine that any man who is now lying out there would like to think that because possibly his friends or relatives had more money than others they were able to erect a better or more magnificent tombstone over his remains than poorer people would be able to put over their sons. I have a brother who died out there, who in his lifetime always looked after his men. That was his chief effort, and the same remark applies to every other officer and non-commissioned officer out there. I know that he thought, and the others would think, that there could be no higher memorial given them, now they are dead, than that they should have the same tombstones as everyone else who fought and fell out there.[8]

Throughout the region, people talked about the war. There was also much talk about what the world would be like once the conflict came to an end. From reading about the discussions that took place in halls across the country, we get an idea of the hopes that were held by people on the home front. Although we do not have a record of what everyone thought, reports like this one about the Great Crosby Literary Society indicate the sort of topics that were being debated. Despite the mention of 'problems' in the title of the talk, the lecture contains a fair amount of optimism about the post-war world. The war offered examples of how the country could be improved. Yet it must be noted that not everyone at this meeting agreed with the speaker's prognosis.

Graves for overseas soldiers, Everton cemetery. (Courtesy of Liverpool Record Office, Liverpool Libraries 352 ENG/2/3282)

The last ordinary meeting of the 1916–17 session was held in St. Faith's Hall on Friday evening, the 9th inst., the Chair being taken by Mr W. H. Jacobsen, President of the society.

A most interesting paper on 'After-the-War Problems' was read by Mr T. W. Smith, a valued member of the society and it was apparent that the gentleman had made a thorough study of the subject. Mr Smith said that in preparing his paper the principal difficulty had been the condensing of his remarks into the short space of time allowed for reading the paper that evening. That there would be criticism of some of his points was inevitable, and he would welcome it, as it would assist in obtaining a proper view of the tremendous issues at stake. The future of our Empire and our race were in the melting-pot. The pitfalls would be many, some of them as yet unforeseen. When peace came he supposed that the aim of our statesmen would be to stimulate the prosperity of the nation so as to remove the evil effects of the war as speedily as possible. To do this we should have to pay more attention to the markets which we already hold, and new ones would have to be created and fostered. The question of wages, presenting many difficulties, would have to be thoroughly gone into. In this connection he ventured to suggest that payment should be made on an entirely new plan. It seemed to him that it was manifestly unfair that the same rate of pay should be given to the single man as to the married man with much greater responsibilities. The principle of this was recognised in the Army by the system of allowances to married men and men with dependants. To some extent we also saw the principle recognised in the abatement (small as it was) of income tax to the man with children dependent on him ... Coming to the question of trade after the war he was disposed to agree with those who thought that there would be a big increase at any rate for some time to come. There was the question of reinstatement of the devastated countries which would provide a large amount of work. Capital had left the belligerent countries for neutral countries rendering them wealthy beyond their wildest dreams and they would be ready to spend their wealth when the opportunity came. The employment of women, he thought, would have to continue as it would be necessary, in view of the war wastage amongst the men. Industries would have to be financed, especially new ones, and in this connection our banking and credit system would have to be radically changed ...[9]

The Liverpool Workers' Industrial Vigilance Committee anticipated problems for demobilised soldiers, particularly those from the lower classes. The first letter below was sent to the National War Emergency Committee to ask for their assistance in order to prevent former soldiers being charged for money they owed to institutions where their children may have been placed during the conflict. These concerns give some idea of the issues that were of importance to the working men who volunteered for the forces in the first months of the war. They were aware of what had happened after the Second Boer War, and wanted to prevent men leaving the army only to find themselves in prison for not having paid fees that had mounted up while they were away. The second letter is from the Home Secretary Reginald McKenna to the National War

Emergency Committee reassuring them that the circumstances had changed and that returning soldiers would have no need to fear charges for non-payment of reformatory school fees.

December 22 1914

Dear Mr Middleton,

My Committee this afternoon instructed me to send you the enclosed resolution ... After the South African War, cases occurred in this city where men who had been at the front <u>were arrested</u> and <u>imprisoned</u> for arrears due in respect to their children in the <u>industrial schools</u>, notwithstanding the fact that their wives had been receiving assistance during their absence from the <u>Transvaal War Fund</u>. Our opinion is that the fees ought not to be paid out of a separation allowance because it is in most cases meagre enough without deductions. We feel that arrears accumulating while the breadwinner is at the front should be cancelled on his return. It is to prevent the recurrence of the previous scandal that we trust the National War Emergency Committee will use its influence with the authorities.

Yours faithfully,

S. Higenbottam.

5 March 1915

Dear Mr Middleton,

You wrote to me on the 18th January about the possibility of men who are serving with His Majesty's Forces and have children in Reformatory or Industrial Schools being summoned on their return to civil life for arrears of payments, which may have accrued due under Orders made upon them by the Courts to contribute towards their children's maintenance. I had already under consideration the position of such parents, and instructions have been issued that men who are serving with His Majesty's Forces shall not be called upon to contribute to the maintenance of their children in Reformatory or Industrial Schools, and any arrears which may accrue under existing Orders will be remitted.

R McKenna.[10]

At the end of the war there was an enormous expression of relief across the nation. Like any other celebration, the festivities that marked the conclusion of the conflict tell us something about the feelings of the people who celebrated. The following newspaper reports from Bootle, Birkenhead and Liverpool respectively tell of people leaving their workplaces and taking to the streets to collectively express their joy. Business, a constant feature of any working day, ceased. With the exception of flag and newspaper sellers, there was little point in attempting to sell anything while the people just wanted to express their joy. Flags were waved, hoisted and hung. The sounds of bells were heard for the first time in many years. In a city where the gathering of large crowds had frequently been associated with social disorder, some journalists noted the good behaviour of the crowds who gathered in the streets. Indeed, the only person getting into any trouble was an effigy of the kaiser.

It came so suddenly. We had all been anxiously awaiting the news, and yet when the word came through at five o'clock this Monday morning when most of us were abed, Germany had signed the Allies' terms for an armistice, there was a moment of doubt. It did not seem possible that in this fashion had come the end – that the long drawn-out agony of four fearful years had indeed ended – that the last gun had been fired – that the last man had fallen in the world's greatest war – that the powers of righteousness had indeed triumphed over the forces of darkness and civilisation was saved to the world ...

The sound of bells was heard, as for the first time in four years the chimes in the tower of Bootle Town Hall were released, and rang out continuously to acclaim the glad news. The flags of the Allies were run up above and around the Town Hall, and the whole town broke out in bunting – flags of Britain, France, Belgium, America, Japan, Italy, Serbia, Portugal. All these were to be seen and more. There was scarcely a house in the borough without its flag – it was really wondrous where they all came from. And some of the humbler streets quite out-flagged some of the decorous thoroughfares dedicated to semi-detached villadom. Litherland-road was a blaze of bunting – Hawthorne-road lost some of its dreariness – the streets off Marsh-lane were resplendent. Plainly all the world and his wife had hunted up their flags or anything that would serve the purpose. In one case an enthusiast had hung out a scarlet banner on which was the inscription in big white letters, 'Peace and Plenty,' and all reading the words must have fervently re-echoed its hope even though the phrase itself smacks somewhat of an election slogan.

Dockland joined in the chorus of jubilation in its own pandemoniac way. 'Letting in the New Year' was nothing to it. Sirens, whistles, ships' bells roared, shrilled, boomed, and tinkled in glad abandon, and factory hooters screamed continuous notes of 'Pip-pip-pip-Peace!' The roads near the docks were filled by cheering, laughing crowds of workers who poured out from munition works, shipyard, factory and workshop, and made a bee-line for their homes. There had evidently been a spontaneous cessation of work. The trams were packed, the trains scarcely less full. Khaki-clad men of the Labour Battalions marched along singing and cheering, and waving flags. Everywhere flags – everywhere flag-wavers. Shops were open, but there was 'nothing doing' unless they happened to be in the flag-selling line, in which case business was brisk enough. But anyhow, shopkeepers didn't want business on this day of all days, and soon began putting up the shutters and joining in the jubilee. It may be safely said that less work was done in Bootle on Monday last than on any other week-day for many a long year. Those who had to, 'carried on' as well as might be. The rest quit. Hundreds flocked into Liverpool, but the thousands that remained in the borough filled the streets with flag-waving, cheering, excited crowds until a late hour in the evening. The youthful populace did their bit with tin-cans and fireworks.

'You are entitled to rejoice,' Mr Lloyd George had said to the jubilant crowd which gathered outside 10 Downing Street that morning. Well, Bootle rejoiced.[11]

'Fight for the freedom of nations.' This is the inscription that was placed over the Shaftesbury Boys' Club active service roll in 1914. The boys assembled before this roll and before the club's laurel roll on Monday evening at a general salute by the bugle band, and the pioneer boys marched past and saluted the 620 names on it. After an hour and a half of boisterous fun and fireworks there was a surprising hush as the boys were told the story of the beginning of enlistment from the club and the steady flow of recruits. Then came the pent-up cheers for 'the boys,' some of whom were present after long service. The proceedings included the National Anthem and contributions for the last despatch of Christmas gifts for the Navy and Army members. All week the club has kept open house and a merry one, and Thomas-street has been made to look like a fairy scene, the decorations, which are a credit to the mother of three soldiers, having been carried out in an artistic scheme that has drawn visitors from far and wide to see it.

The week has been given over to rejoicings on a generous scale in celebration of the cessation of hostilities. The 'Birkenhead News' was on Monday the first to give the town official intimation to the public that the armistice terms had been agreed to and signed by Germany, and within a few minutes of the announcement the syrens [sic] and works hooters made known the glad information to the people at large. Almost at once the scene that presented itself was one of the utmost joy and thankfulness, all carried out, it is pleasing to state, with the most complete orderliness and good humour. As the day advanced the streets became thronged with rejoicing crowds, workmen having ceased operations, shops and offices closed, and a general holiday taken to commemorate the great occasion. It is worthy of note that not a single charge of over-indulgence was recorded by the police, the conduct of the crowds throughout the period being admirable.

The 'holiday' spirit soon became infectious on Monday, when it was known that the employees in the big yards, etc., were 'out' for the rest of the day. In some of the Corporation departments a good many of the men took a holiday from about noon, and in the tramways department the result was that no cars were running during the afternoon and evening. It appears that the early morning shift of drivers and girl conductors worked on until their time ended, but the relief shift that should then have gone on decided to join in the general holiday and took 'French leave.' The conductors, it is said, were the most clamorous for release from duty, seeing that thousands of other girls were joyously

Armistice decorations, Birkenhead. (Author's collection)

parading the streets; but whether that was the case or not, it is a fact that work was dropped, and no cars were run. Fortunately, the day was beautifully fine, and the public took the absence of cars very tolerantly.[12]

The Prime Minister made the great announcement at 10.20 am in London. Within a minute later the 'Echo,' which had everything in readiness, was on sale in the streets of Liverpool giving the tremendous news for which the whole world had been waiting for days.

The papers were bought up feverishly, but for a time there was no excitement beyond cheering by the waiting newsboys and a small crowd.

People wanted to make sure; besides, four years of sternly pent-up feeling could not be released in a moment. As the news spread in the city, flags were hoisted on the public buildings, and then cheer after cheer broke out from the gradually-increasing crowds in the streets, and every soldier and sailor was enthusiastically greeted.

Some of the newsboys were literally swept off their feet. Men rushed into shops and cafes, flourishing the paper and shouting out the good news.

There was much hand-shaking between friend and stranger. Everybody was a brother in joy …

In the central thoroughfares – Lord-street, Church-street and vicinity – jubilation was the keynote of everyone's actions. The business places, at any rate up to midday, remained open, but no trading was done; the fact was the public were in no mood to buy anything, not even food. At the windows and doors of the shops the assistants were congregated and joined the congested stream of pedestrians in the shouts of joy which from time to time rent the air.

Of flags of all the Allied nations there was a lavish display from nearly every window, and hundreds of people carried small Union Jacks in their hands and waved them in ecstasy over their heads.

The American Y.M.C.A. depot, in Lord-street was the centre of extraordinary enthusiasm. British and United States soldiers and sailors united in adding to the merriment of the occasion.

It was with difficulty the tramcars were able to creep slowly through the crowded streets. As the forenoon wore on the streets became packed with people. Although, as stated above, the business houses were not closed at midday, there was a general feeling that they could not long remain open.

The first intimation of the good news which reached the river was the hoisting of flags by the stage masters. This was between 10.30 and 10.35, and immediately the significance of the display was grasped by the commanders of the river craft, flags were broken at every masthead and steam sirens 'cock-a-doodle-dooed' in raucous discord …

'It seems too good to be true,' was the remark of a reflective man of middle age, who stood reading his 'Echo' at the corner of Lime-street and London-road. The young people, however, had no manner of doubt as to the truth of the tidings. A procession of university students passed by singing gaily, and they were soon followed by bands of women workers and school children, all taking up the refrain of victory. Flag-sellers carried on a brisk business, and in the bright sunshine the leading thoroughfares soon presented masses of moving colour.

'What has become of the old Kaiser and his Junkers?' was the question often asked, the successive telegrams being scanned keenly for news of the fate of the authors of the four years' war …

Programme for the peace celebrations in Newton in Makerfield. (Courtesy of Mr Geoffrey Sim, St Helens Local History and Archives Library NPC/3/4/3/9)

Some amusement was caused when the figure of the ex-Kaiser, in the custody of a smiling British policeman, was driven through the streets of Liverpool. The All-Lowest wore his full war apparel, inclusive of the Iron Cross and a shining headpiece, but he wore an air of dejection. Near the American Y.M.C.A. he and his custodian got out of their car for a few minutes, and were jostled by a big crowd of spectators, who urged the mimic Wilhelm to 'hold his hands up.' 'We're going to burn the guy tomorrow night,' said one of the Yankees.[13]

For many the end of the war involved a transition from military to civilian life. The main concern for returning men was work. Even those who found work could experience a reduction of their income. Some were unable to return to the jobs they had left, while others could walk into the positions they had held before the war. The demobilisation scheme has been described as 'somewhat bizarre', because men were released as individuals not as military units.[14] This was an effort to avoid a spike in unemployment. The men who worked in the most essential trades were the first to be released.

No fewer than 89,000 soldiers will eventually be demobilised in Liverpool. The Employment Exchanges are already making arrangements to reabsorb them into industry as speedily as possible, and employers are being asked to claim men they wish to return to their service, as well as to indicate their prospective labour requirements when they are able to resume full peace-time activity ...

Before the general dissolution commences, it is expected that a generous leave will be given to the volunteers, of which there may be no shortage, who re-engage to serve in the new Regular Army.

Concentration centres in France will serve the various dispersal stations that are being set up in this country. Liverpool men, for instance, will be collected at a certain town over the Channel, and then will be transferred in batches to Litherland. Here each soldier will receive a protection card, a railway warrant to his home, a ration book, a six months' free out-of-work endowment policy, and a cash payment.

Concerning the last-named, it will take the form of an instalment of any credit to his account, his military pay and allowances for a month's furlough, a grant for the purchase of civilian clothes, and any service gratuity. Further instalments will be forwarded during the following three weeks through the post. He will then be sent home on four weeks' furlough, at the end of which he will be finally demobilised, though not necessarily discharged.

Seeing that he remains a soldier, a man will be entitled to wear his uniform during this period, but afterwards he should have donned civilian garb. He surrenders his arms and equipment at the dispersal station, and he must hand in his greatcoat at the end of the month, but the khaki uniform itself is to become his private property. Not without interest, moreover, is the suggestion that he should be given his steel helmet as well, and certainly these quaint battle-scarred relics would be treasured heirlooms in many a family.[15]

It is difficult to gauge the effects of the war on the soldiers and sailors who returned to civilian roles after the conflict. Their experiences of the war will have varied, as would the homes they returned to. Yet in one way or another all would have been influenced by the conflict. This unpublished essay by Percy Douglas, who served with the Liverpool Scottish before joining the Royal Flying Corps, addresses the topic of humour. Other items that were deposited with this essay, such as *The Best 500 Cockney War Stories*, indicate Douglas's interest in the funny side of the war. Even so, his ruminations on humour had a serious edge. In the light of war, domestic troubles appear trivial and should raise a smile rather than a scowl.

How much easier and more pleasant life would be for all of us if we were all endowed with this priceless gift – a sense of humour.

Fortunately, this gift does form part of the mental make-up of the majority of people; some of course possessing it in a greater degree than others.

Anyone who was at the front during the Great War will agree that it was only 'the sense of humour' of the majority of the troops that made existence in that hell on earth at all possible, and further than that it undoubtedly saved many from losing their mental balance. Blessed was the man who could always see the funny side, and what a boon it was to his immediate fellow. It is the little things in life that so often irritate us beyond measure, and yet if we but stop and analyse these petty annoyances how really silly and futile they appear.

Look around, and we will find that the happy people (and who doesn't want to be happy) are the individuals with this trait in their character. It is the key to happiness in married life. How many marriages are failures through lack of it. He in a frivolous moment ... jumps over the garden fence to retrieve the child's ball, and in the process falls and tears his trousers on an unexpected nail. She calls him a fool, and tells him he ought to know better, and further he has ruined the garment. And, anyhow he could have gone round by the gate. Alas, poor woman, she has failed to see how silly he looked when he fell, and what an absurd expression his face wore at the moment. Therein lies a tragedy; and simply because she failed to see the funny side. As a result she not only makes herself miserable, but the unfortunate husband and child as well when the whole affair might have been a cause of general amusement for all concerned.

Who are the men and women who are always grousing about their lot, who lack friends, who are ... indulging in that pernicious and well nigh incurable habit of self-pity; why, the ones who can never see the funny side of life.

Don't take everything so seriously – a matter of life and death. After all there is always a comical side to most things, if we will but look for it.

Cultivate this art, and you will find that the wheels of life run much more smoothly than you once thought. In fact your whole mental attitude will broaden and you will not only make yourself happier, but your fellow creatures will appreciate you too.[16]

Before Field Marshall Douglas Haig visited Liverpool on 5 July 1919 and received the freedom of the city, there had been much debate in the *Liverpool Daily Post* about a suitable date for the event and the most appropriate way to mark the day.

The Bishop of Liverpool, Francis Chavasse, thought that it was inappropriate for the general to be greeted on a Sunday. Others preferred Sunday. In the end, Saturday was chosen. Aside from the question of when it should take place, there was discussion about why so many ex-soldiers appeared to be unwilling to participate in the march. Among the reasons put forward was reluctance to sign-up to take part in the event because of the 'fruit of certain Army experiences'. Although the paper stressed that these objections were not the result of a lack of patriotism, such attitudes indicate that some ex-soldiers did not have a very positive view of the army.

The Bishop of Liverpool, acting on behalf of himself and the Liverpool Diocesan Chapter, voices a strong objection to the proposal to hold the forthcoming military parade in Liverpool on a Sunday. In a communication which he has sent to the commanding officer of the Western Command he pleads for a transfer of the event to a week-day on the grounds that a Sunday spectacle will entail much extra labour, will tend to secularise the Sabbath, and will deeply wound the religious feelings of a multitude of citizens. The letter is as follows:

'The Palace. Liverpool June 20th, 1919.

Dear Sir, At a meeting of the Liverpool Diocesan Chapter, consisting of the two bishops, archdeacons, canons, rural deans, and proctors in Convocation, held at this house yesterday, I was requested to write to you in their name with regard to the march past of 40,000 men arranged for the afternoon of Sunday, July 6th. It was unanimously agreed that the military authorities should be asked to transfer the review to a week-day. We represent the Church of England in South-West Lancashire, and we feel sure that we have the support of tens of thousands of Christian people belonging to other religious bodies. We make the request on three grounds:

I: Because the march past will involve a large amount of Sunday labour, and will deprive many of our fellow-citizens of their much-needed Sunday rest. Sunday labour means irreligion, discontent, and diminished physical vitality.

2: Because it will tend to secularise Sunday. It will set a precedent which will be largely followed. It will strike a blow at the moral and spiritual welfare of our people. It was a saying of Voltaire that if you would destroy Christianity you must first kill Sunday. It will turn a day of quiet, rest, and worship into a day of turmoil, excitement, and business. It was the soul of the British nation that won the war, and a secularised Sunday lowers the national tone and materialises the national spirit.

3: Because it will deeply wound the religious feelings of a great multitude of our best citizens. The men and women who value Sunday have done much to win the war. They have set an example of self-sacrifice, fortitude, and comradeship to the nation. They have freely given their money, their time, and their children to help their country – very many of them are mourning their dead. They desire to greet the 40,000 gallant men who have come back from the front, and the great Commander-in-Chief, whose high Christian character has won their admiration as much as his brilliant generalship. And they are debarred because the review is held on Sunday.

We are aware of the difficulties involved in the change of date. But a great principle is at stake, and we most earnestly ask the military authorities to take the necessary steps to transfer this great military spectacle to a week-day.'[17]

We understand that, considered in one important aspect, the preparations for the forthcoming Victory March of Liverpool's ex-soldiers have not proved entirely satisfactory to the promoters of the scheme. The success of the Victory March and civic welcome must depend almost entirely on the way in which the mobilised men regard the matter. There is no evidence to show that the ex-service men of Liverpool have been very eager to take part in the proceedings on occasion of Sir Douglas Haig's visit. The completed register for the march is said to show a fairly satisfactory total of names, but if an extension of time for registering had not been made, our information is that the list would have been a total of under 4,000.

Demobilised men, in explaining their objection to the Victory March and civic reception, say that the register itself was a mistake. Those who underwent military service will readily understand the objection an ex-service man feels to registering his name in connection with any fresh military or quasi-military engagement. His objections have nothing to do with patriotism or anything of that nature. Simply, they are the fruit of certain Army experiences. It is a fact that several men have expressed a fear that the Victory March register would be used later in connection with the reconstruction of the Territorial Force. The authorities already have their records, and such a fear is, of course, groundless; but it exists. It is thought, however, that many men who have fought shy of the resister will turn up at the points of rendezvous on the day of the march, impelled by a spirit of esprit de corps.

An objection is raised to the change of the day of the march from Sunday to Saturday. Whatever the victory march may be to the spectators, to the men taking part it involves much of the discomfort of any ordinary route march. There are likely to be tedious periods of waiting. For the sake of the object of the march these men say that they might have been willing to undergo one more route march on Sunday. But after a morning's work and with the prospect of hurried journeys to and from town a Saturday afternoon march is a different thing.

In any case, demobilised men are expressing very warmly their feelings with regard to the change of day, particularly the reason for the change. They do not hesitate to recall the days when Sunday frequently meant greater war horrors and more strenuous work than any other day of the week, and they speak of the religious ministrations and experiences far different on one and the same Sunday. The words of a Liverpool man who is closely in touch with demobilised soldiers rather clearly express their view. 'The Victory March,' he said 'would consecrate Sunday, July 6th, not desecrate it.'

One other thing should be mentioned, because demobilised men are talking about it. The ex-soldiers are to parade either in khaki or in civilian clothes. It does not matter which, but the men are certain that ex-officers will parade in full regimental dress, and they feel that the march will have an atmosphere of military discipline and distinction. This objection is small in its way, but it is as well to know that these things are in the minds of the demobilised men, and that those who have doffed their khaki are saying them.

The Lord Mayor has received several requests that employers should be asked to give facilities to demobilised men to leave their employment early on Saturday next to enable them to take part in the parade. He trusts that, as far as is compatible with business, this request will be granted.[18]

Both of he following extracts are attempts to make sense of the war. Howard Cochran's short piece entitled 'Hate' was part of a collection of essays and other items published by staff who worked at the Postal Censor's Office in Liverpool. As soon as victory was declared, theories about why Germany was defeated were proposed, rebuffed and amended. Some of the popular explanations are referred to below. After respectfully dismissing each reason, Howard Cochran's piece assumes a more serious tone. Not only does he resent Germany, he despises Germany. Cochran seems to be returning Germany's 'Hymn of Hate' after having added his own venomous verses. His comment about Germany not remaining Germany is puzzling. It may, however, be a reflection on the political turmoil in the country during 1918–1919. The second extract, an anonymous poem, appeared in a book marking the centenary of the Liverpool Chamber of Commerce in 1950. Like Cochran, the poet reflects on Germany but directs his anger at the leaders of the country instead of the nation as a whole.

Has it ever struck you, old dears, how we won this war? Oh, I know you'll get on your hind legs, at once, and, well primed by the newspapers, an' public opinion, an' all that kind o' tosh, you'll yell at the top of your little voices:

THE BRITISH NAVY

And you won't be far wrong either, but you'll be wrong all the same, old dears.

Don't – for the Lord's sake – think I'm belittling in any way the perfectly topping work the dear Old Navy has put in.

I'm not – not for the ghost of a second.

Others of you, who've been in khaki (jolly good luck too!), or who've had relations, or pals, who have been in khaki, will screech – equally loudly:

THE BRITISH ARMY

They, also, are well off the map!

The British Army's work has been as absolutely top-hole as the British Navy's work. But it's neither the British Army nor the British Navy that's won this war.

You, Sir, or you, Madam, have once crossed the Atlantic, or have had a cocktail at the Adelphi – or perhaps (how wonderful!) have actually met an American officer – you'll say:

AMERICA

… But you're wrong, too.

America – let's own it at once – put the finishing touch to an almost completed picture.

But America did not win the war.

Neither did France, nor Italy, nor Greece, nor Serbia, nor Romania, nor Japan, nor China, nor even Russia!

Got you guessing?

Thought I had – GERMANY won this war!

But not for the happy Fatherland – dear me, no! – for us, every allied son and daughter of us!

Germany won this war by her 'Hymn of Hate'!

For hate implies two things: – (l) Respect. (2) Fear.

And – thank God! – neither you, nor I, nor any of us, ever respected or feared Germany.

If we'd done either we couldn't have managed either the Battle of Jutland, the Retreat from Mons, or recovered after the Cambrai set-back.

Why did we manage?

The 'Hymn of Hate'!

We *despised* Germany – and we shall go on despising Germany as long as Germany remains Germany.

Fortunately, Germany will not remain Germany very much longer.

Germany won this war for the Allies from the very moment her 'Hymn of Hate' was penned.[19]

It might be fitting to end this phase of the Chamber's experience by quoting a poem written by an employee of a member of the Chamber who, serving in France and finding his demobilisation unduly delayed, appeared to obtain some relief from boredom by a question which to this day has not been answered.

'I WONDER?

I wonder if, when Armageddon's over
And glorious peace once more will reign,
Munition workers still will be in clover
With feather beds, and strawberries and cream.
I wonder if they'll still be earning weekly
What to a soldier would be annual wealth;
Or if they'll turn to their pre-war jobs meekly,
Without a holiday, even for their health.

I wonder if the women in the city
Working so hard, so late (poor things!) in banks
And offices, etcetera (what a pity
That they should get such little grudging thanks!)
Will, with a noble patriotic gesture,
Resign their jobs *and* salaries, and then
Be seen once more clad in domestic vesture
Pushing a pram and not a fountain pen.

I wonder if the host of Whitehall Workers –
S.O.'s. P.M.'s, M.P.'s, and O.B.E.'s
And all those who have been accused as shirkers,
Will be hard at it after years of peace.
For instance, will Victoria be thronging
With multitudes of red-capped F.M.P.'s,
Dreaming of days gone by, the days belonging
To times of passes, 'stead of 'seasons please?'

I wonder whether Germany, defeated,
A bankrupt nation, hated by the world.
And finding that she's been so badly cheated
And into utter desperation hurled,
Will turn and rend her once revered Kaiser,
Will Soldier Schmidt, who comes from Wittenburg,
Or Fritz from Berlin now a little wiser,
Knock bullets 'stead of nails in Hindenburg!
I wonder![20]

Even before the war ended, there had been a shift towards state assistance for the construction of houses. The principle that only private business should build houses had been undermined. A Housing Act in 1919 set an ambitious goal of half a million houses by the early 1920s. A downturn in the economy meant that the 'homes for heroes' were never as plentiful as had been anticipated. The housing situation on Merseyside was particularly poor with families with little wherewithal remaining in private, rented accommodation throughout the inter-war years.[21] Eleanor Rathbone's letter about the opportunity to use prefabricated buildings that had been raised by the British and American military in Knotty Ash captures the sense of urgency felt by those who were interested in the welfare of the less prosperous portion of the population.

Sir, It is important that the public should recognise the full significance of the fiasco that has occurred in the matter of the Knotty Ash huts. As explained in your columns by the chairman of the Housing Committee, the committee have been endeavouring for the past month to obtain from the Government the necessary sanction and the equally necessary guarantees of financial aid to enable them to purchase the whole of these huts, those contained both in the American and British camps, for temporary housing purposes. Until a few days ago they had approved warmly of the scheme, provided that certain necessary precautions were taken. There is no reason to believe that the Central Authority has changed its mind in this respect.

But within less than a week of the date when the American huts, which are by far the larger portion, are to be put up to public auction it has been sprung upon the committee that conditions would be exacted making it a practical impossibility to proceed with the scheme, unless, indeed, by purchasing the whole site from its various owners for permanent use as a housing area – a transaction which, whatever its merits, could not be accomplished within three days. Further, the expected financial guarantees are indefinitely postponed.

It is not clear to what extent the difficulties could have been averted by the Government consistently with its responsibilities towards the United States authorities. But what is clear is that these difficulties ought to have been made known to the committee at an earlier date, when there might have been time to find a way of escape by negotiation. It must be obvious to any outsider that the huts are worth more to the Housing Committee than they can be to any other purchaser, since no one else is in a position to make use of them on their present sites, and so evade the great cost of transport and re-erection. As Americans are usually credited with being keen men of business, it is difficult to believe that no bargain could have been struck with them if the difficulty had been made known to the committee at an earlier stage. As it is, unless some extraordinary step is taken by the Government, the Liverpool public must be prepared to see the destruction within ten days of several hundred potential dwelling-houses which might otherwise have been ready for occupation at least three months before the first brick house can be erected under the Housing Act.

There are those for whom the delay of a few months, more or less, seems a small matter. Comfortably housed in their own suburban dwellings they are content to sneer at wooden huts and to draw enticing pictures of the well-planned and substantial houses that are to be provided by public effort some day, as soon as the infinite leisureliness of bureaucratic procedure permits. Meantime, a considerable proportion of our population, including thousands of returned soldiers, to whom

Prefabricated housing at Knotty Ash, 1920. (Courtesy of Liverpool Record Office, Liverpool Libraries 352 ENG/2/6812)

promises of a 'better England' were so lavishly made, are living under conditions of indescribable discomfort.

A worker for the local War Pensions Committee.[22]

The economic problems facing Merseyside after the war were outlined in a book about British ports by Sanford Darley Cole published in 1923. Liverpool depended on trade, and a number of factors conspired to reduce the amount of trade that passed through the port. Some of these were simply the consequence of readjustments after the war. Others, Cole argues, were the result of the port's reputation for congestion and relatively high charges. The celebrant who displayed the banner declaring 'Peace and Plenty' in Bootle to mark the end of the war would soon be disappointed by the absence of plenty. In more than one respect, peace came at a cost.

The expansion of trade which went on in Liverpool up to the outbreak of war was all sound business. During the war the port was heavily congested with traffic, but the same description of sound business can hardly be applied to what was done then. A great deal of trade was diverted by Government action from ports on the East and South Coasts to Liverpool. Whatever good purpose the activities of the port at the time served – and there has been no lack of laudatory reference since – they also had the effect of giving Liverpool a bad name, for traders became accustomed to connecting congestion and delay with the Mersey port, and this association has remained in the minds of many of them. This may in part account for the depression during the last few years. Whereas the pre-war weight of Liverpool's foreign imports was over 7,000,000 tons per year, in 1921 they were less than 5,500,000 tons. In 1922 the figure was about 5,600,000 tons.

A factor influencing recent and current conditions at Liverpool has been, no doubt, the amount of the port charges. Liverpool was the last to put up charges, and it has been found difficult, at a time of reduced trade and with questions of deferred repairs and renewals claiming attention, to decide what course would be best. Though the Board is not concerned with making profits, it had to pay its way. Nevertheless, as above indicated, a reduction has been made.

Pending reduction of charges, the port, in competition with other centres, apparently lost ground. The relative dearness of Liverpool is alleged to have caused transference of business to other ports, and in particular to Hull. Corn, wool, and transhipment trades were specially affected.

Turning from cargo to passenger traffic, it will be recalled that it was during the war period that the very large passenger steamers were transferred to Southampton for transport purposes. Now these larger boats engaged in the Atlantic passenger traffic have deserted Liverpool in favour of the English Channel port.

In any case, however, a heavy share of the shipping business of the largest and most important industrial district in the country goes through Liverpool. It is sometimes said that the growth of Liverpool is due to its standing on one of the finest natural harbours we have, and to the improvements made in the harbour having attracted shipping. No doubt, without the Mersey Liverpool would never have advanced to its present position, but trade would never have come to the Mersey had not the country round, being a coal area, become covered with populous manufacturing towns, and had not this district become (its climate being favourable) the home of the cotton trade. Liverpool itself is not a place of extensive manufactures, and owes its importance not so much to the Mersey as to the character of the district around it.[23]

One of the many men who fell on hard times during the depression was Thomas O'Neill, a carter from Liverpool who had served in the army before the outbreak of war. He was injured on the Western Front and lost a lung during the war. His descendants remember being told that O'Neill had been a sergeant in the army but lost a stripe when he refused to shoot a man who he believed was innocent. At a time when the depression was at its worst, O'Neill wrote a letter to the MP Clement Attlee asking whether he could offer him any assistance. O'Neill had served with Attlee in the South Lancashire Regiment.

6th May 32

My dear O'Neill

Many thanks for your letter. I am so sorry to hear that you are out of a job, its true of too many in these days, I fear. Unfortunately I don't know anyone to whom I could recommend you. I wish I did. If I hear of any down in Liverpool I will let you know. Remember if you come to London or I come to Liverpool to look me up again.

All the best

Sincerely

C R Atlee[24]

This letter was sent from 79 Blantyre Road, Wavertree, on 19 January 1919. Its author, Eric, was writing to his father, Albert James Butling who was a private in the Army Service Corps. The letters written by Eric and his brother George, who were respectively fourteen and sixteen in 1919, provide a view of the war from the perspective of teenage boys. Both Eric and George

Request for help – Thomas O'Neill.
(Courtesy of Tom Carlin)

had spent their earliest years in Birmingham, where their father was an 'indoor postman'. So when they moved north, the children must have been excited by the prospect of living near the coast. The letter records the two brothers' adventures in the docks. Both before and after his account of their escapade, Eric expresses the hope that his father will soon return. Albert James Butling died of dysentery in May 1919.[25]

Dear Dad

Just a few lines to let you know how things are going on in 'Blighty'. Hoping you are quite well, I can safely answer for ourselves. Mother and George have gone to church and will soon be home having been gone some time. Mr Laidler has come back for good having been demobilised just recently and I hope you will have the same good fortune before long … On Saturday George and I went down town hoping to see the surrender of the German fleet but on arriving there found it was not done. So we went to the Docks but were disappointed because

Figure of grieving child on Liverpool Cenotaph, St George's Plateau. (Author's collection)

we could [not] get in. But we went along a back alley and got in and saw the German sub. Next we inspected a destroyer where they were weighing potato rations. After going down umpteen effluvious alleys we came back to the destroyer which was in dry dock. Next to it was a barge into which we descended but finding nothing in it we ascended and made our way home. That is all the news I have for now Dad. So God bless you hoping you will soon be home.

I remain you ever loving son

Eric.[26]

Notes

Introduction

1 Tony Lane, *Liverpool: City of the Sea* (Liverpool: Liverpool University Press, 1997), p. 14.

2 Sheila Marriner, *The Economic and Social Development of Merseyside* (London: Croom Helm, 1982), p. 142.

3 Francois Crouzet, *The Victorian Economy* (London: Routledge, 1982), p. 97.

4 Mike Stammers, *Liverpool: The Port and its Ships* (Stroud: Alan Sutton 1991), p. 29.

5 A. J. Tennent, *British Merchant Ships Sunk by U-boats in World War One* (Penzance: Periscope Publishing, 2006), pp. 172–173.

6 Mrs Humphry Ward, *England's Effort: Six Letters to an American Friend* (London: Smith, Elder and Co., 1916), pp. 39–40.

7 Sam Davies, '"Crisis? What Crisis?": The National Rail Strike of 1911 and the State Response', *Historical Studies in Industrial Relations*, vol. 33 (2012), p. 106.

8 Marij Van Halmond, *Votes for Women: The Events on Merseyside, 1870–1928* (Liverpool: National Museums and Galleries, 1991), p. 60.

9 Graeme Milne, 'Maritime City, Maritime Culture? Representing Liverpool's Waterfront Districts since the Mid-nineteenth Century', in Mike Benbough-Jackson and Sam Davies (eds), *Merseyside: Culture and Place* (Newcastle: Cambridge Scholars, 2011), pp. 88–108.

10 *Liverpool Echo*, 24 March 1914.

11 Helen B. McCartney, *Citizen Soldiers: The Liverpool Territorials in the First World War* (Cambridge: Cambridge University Press, 2005); and Mike Finn, 'Local Heroes: War News and the Construction of Community in Liverpool, 1914–1918', *Historical Research*, vol. 83, no. 221 (2010), p. 520 –538; Lee P. Ruddin, the "Firsts" world war: A History of the Morale of Liverpudlians as told through Letters to Liverpool Editors, 1915–1918', *International Journal of Regional and Local History*, vol.9, no.2 (2014), pp.79–93.

12 Stephen McGrael, *Wirral in the Great War* (Barnsley: Pen and Sword, 2014); Anthony Hogan, *Merseyside at War* (Stroud: Amberley, 2014)

1 Men and the War

1 Ian F. W. Beckett, 'The nation in arms, 1914–1918', in Ian F. W. Beckett and Ian Sampson (eds), *The Nation in Arms: A Social Study of the British Army in the First World War* (Manchester: Manchester University Press, 1985), p. 7.

2 *Liverpool Echo*, 25 August 1914.

3 David French, *British Strategy and War Aims, 1914–1916* (London: Allen and Unwin, 1986), p. 13.

4 *Great Speeches of the War* (London: Hazel, Watson and Viney, 1915), pp. 282–283.

5 Jill Knight, *The Civil Service Rifles in the Great War: 'All Bloody Gentlemen'* (Barnsley: Pen and Sword, 2004), p. 29.

6 *House of Commons: Parliamentary Debates* (London: Her Majesty's Stationary Office, 1914), 26 November 1914, vol. 68 cc1340-1W.

7 *Liverpool Echo*, 8 August 1914.

8 *Garston and Woolton Weekly News*, 8 January 1915.

9 Nicoletta F. Gullace, *The Blood of Our Sons: Men, Women, and the Renegotiation of British Citizenship during the Great War* (London: Palgrave, 2002), p. 36.

10 *Liverpool Courier*, 18 August 1914.

11 *Sphinx: Guild of Undergraduates University of Liverpool*, vol. 22, no. 1 (November 1914), p.32.

12 *Young Crescent: Near and Far*, vol. 3, no.10 (October 1917), p. 3.

13 *Young Crescent: Near and Far*, vol. 3, no. 11 (November 1917), p. 6.

14 *Young Crescent: Near and Far*, vol. 4, no. 8 (August 1918), p. 5.

15 Stephen Badsey, *The British Army in Battle and its Image 1914–1918* (London: Continuum, 2009), p. 42.

16 Peter Barham, *Forgotten Lunatics of the Great War* (New Haven: Yale University Press, 2004).

17 *Liverpool Daily Post*, 15 January 1915.

18 Tony Ashworth, *Trench Warfare: The Live and Let Live System* (London: Macmillan, 1980).

19 *Liverpool Echo*, 14 March 1917.

20 *Formby and Crosby Times*, 17 April 1915.

21 Jessica Meyers, *Men of War: Masculinity and the First World War* (London: Macmillan, 2009), p. 47.

22 Wirral Archives, Herbert Adams Diaries, YPX/27/2 (1916).

23 Trudi Tate, *Modernism, History and the First World War* (Manchester: Manchester University Press, 1998), p. 5.

24 *The British Citizen and Empire Worker*, 13 January 1917, p. 20.

25 *The Sphinx: Being the official organ of the 6th Battalion Manchester Regiment*, vol. I, no. 3 (May 1915), p. 3.

26 Emrys Hughes, *Sydney Silverman: Rebel in Parliament* (London: Skilton, 1969).

27 *Evening Express*, 1 November 1916.

28 Liverpool Maritime Museum Archives, Royal Liverpool Seaman's Orphan Institution, Correspondence regarding staff appointment, D/SO/12/1/18.

29 *Bootle Times*, 3 May 1918.

30 Constance Alsop, *The Life of James W. Alsop LL.D, B.A.* (Liverpool: University Press of Liverpool, 1926), pp. 199–201.

31 Imperial War Museum, DS/Misc/49, pp. 38–39.

32 Robert Crossley, *Olaf Stapledon: Speaking for the Future* (Liverpool: Liverpool University Press, 1994), pp. 131–132.

33 Olaf Stapledon, 'Experiences in the Friends' Ambulance Unit', in Julian Bell (ed.), *We did not fight: 1914–1918 Experiences of War Resisters* (London: Coben-Sanderson, 1935), pp. 371–374.

34 Matthew Hughes, *Allenby and British Strategy in the Middle East, 1917–1919* (London: Frank Cass, 1999), p. 41.

35 *Birkenhead News*, 2 February 1918.

36 Tim Cook, 'Grave Beliefs: Stories of the Supernatural and the Uncanny among Canada's Great War Trench Soldiers', *Journal of Military History*, vol. 77, no. 2 (2013), pp. 521–542.

37 Tommy Kehoe, *The Fighting Mascot: The True Story of a Boy Soldier* (London: Blackie and Son, 1919), pp. 53–55.

38 Michael Snape, *God and the British Soldier: Religion and the British Army in the Era of the Two World Wars* (London: Routledge, 2005), p. 48.

39 *Liverpool Catholic Herald*, 13 November 1915.
40 William Abbott Herdman, *George Andrew Herdman, 1895–1916: The record of a short but strenuous life* (Liverpool: privately printed, 1917), pp. 97–98, 104.
41 *Deeside Advertiser*, 11 May 1917.
42 *Sphinx: Guild of Undergraduates University of Liverpool*, 22:1 (November 1914), p. 4.
43 Paul Fussell, *The Great War and Modern Memory* (London: Oxford University Press, 1977), p. 235.
44 Jay Winter, 'Paris, London, Berlin 1914–1919: Capital Cities at War', in Jay Winter and Jean-Louis Robert (eds), *Capital Cities at War: Paris, London, Berlin 1914–1919, vol. 1* (Cambridge: Cambridge University Press, 1997), p. 6.
45 *Wallasey News*, 28 November 1914.
46 'Liverpool Merchants' Mobile Hospital', *British Medical Journal*, vol. 1, no. 2825 (1915), p. 354.
47 John. D. Hayward, *The Liverpool Merchants' Hospital in France* (Liverpool: Daily Post, 1919), pp. 48–49.
48 Liddle Collection (Leeds University Library), WWI/ANZAC/Aust/028.
49 Hugh Durnford, et al., *Escapers All* (London: J. Lane, 1932).
50 Walter Duncan, *How I Escaped from Germany* (Liverpool: Edward Howell, 1919), pp. 91–95.
51 Liddle Collection (Leeds University Library), WWI/AIR/ 204.
52 *Garston and Woolton Weekly News*, 25 June 1915.
53 *Birkenhead and Cheshire Advertiser*, 17 July 1915.
54 Imperial War Museum, Edward Hillison, 9581.
55 Denis Winter, *Deaths Men: Soldiers of the Great War* (London: Allen Lane, 1978), p. 147.
56 Rachel Duffett, *The Stomach for Fighting: Food and Soldiers of the Great War* (Manchester: Manchester University Press, 2012), p. 180.
57 Liverpool Record Office, 920/BEH/3/2.

2 Women and the War

1 Samuel Hynes, *A War Imagined: The First World War and English Culture* (New York: Atheneum, 1991), p. 88.
2 *Liverpool Daily Post*, 9 February 1918.
3 Ian J. Cawood and David McKinnon-Bell, *The First World War* (London: Routledge, 2001), p. 67.

4 Kenneth Burnely and Guy Huntington (eds), *Images of Wirral: a celebration in words and photographs of a unique peninsula* (Heswall: Silver Birch Press ,1991), no page numbers.

5 Liverpool Record Office, 920 ROC, pp.1–5.

6 Krista Cowman, *Mrs Brown is a Man and a Brother: Women in Merseyside's Political Organisations, 1890–1920* (Liverpool: Liverpool University Press, 2004), pp. 149–50.

7 Liverpool Civic Service League, *Report of Work done during the war, August, 1914 –January, 1915* (Liverpool: Civic Service League 1915), pp.15–18.

8 *Liverpool Echo*, 6 July 1917.

9 *Ellesmere Port Advertiser*, 20 October 1915.

10 *Statistics of the Military Effort of the British Empire During the Great War*, 1914–1920 (London: HMSO, 1922), p. 505.

11 *Liverpool Daily Post*, 29 September 1916.

12 Lucy Delap, Maria DiCenzo, Leila Ryan 'Introduction' in Lucy Delap, Maria DiCenzo, Leila Ryan (eds), *Feminism and the Periodical Press, 1900–1918, Vol. 1* (London: Routledge, 2006), p. xxxvii.

13 *Bootle Times*, 9 Feb 1917.

14 *Liverpool Daily Post*, 15 October 1914.

15 Clare Debenham, *Birth Control and the Rights of Women: Post-suffrage Feminism in the Early Twentieth Century* (London: I.B. Tauris, 2014), p. 173.

16 Ivy A. Ireland, *Margaret Beavan of Liverpool: Her character and work* (Liverpool: Henry Young & Sons Ltd., 1938), pp. 88-89.

17 Leonore Davidoff, 'The Separation of Home and Work? Landladies and Lodgers in nineteenth- and Twentieth-Century England', in Sandra Burman (ed.), *Fit Work for Women* (London: Croom Helm, 1979), p. 90.

18 *Garston and Woolton Weekly News*, 25 June 1915.

19 *Liverpool Daily Post*, 15 August 1915.

20 *Young Crescent: Near and Far*, vol. 2, no. 6 (June 1916), p. 3.

21 Agnes Cowper, *A Backward Glance on Merseyside* (Birkenhead: Willmer Bros,1948), pp. 104–106.

22 *Birkenhead and Cheshire Advertiser*, 17 March 1916.

23 Paul Ward, *Britishness Since 1870* (London: Psychology Press, 2004), p. 40.

24 *Liverpool Daily Post*, 4 July 1917.

25 *Liverpool Echo*, 3 July 1917.

26 Liddle Collection (Leeds University Library), WW1/WO/098.

27 Sharon Ouditt, *Fighting Forces, Writing Women: Identity and Ideology in the First World War* (London: Routledge, 1994), p. 27.

28 Thekla Bowser, *The Story of British V.A.D. Work in the Great War* (London: A. Melrose, 1917), pp. 74–76.

29 Christine E. Hallett, *Veiled Warriors: Allied Nurses of the First World War* (Oxford: Oxford University Press, 2014), p. 55.

30 *Liverpool Courier*, 11 Jan 1915.

31 Liverpool Maritime Museum Archives, DX/186/87.

32 Liddle Collection (Leeds University Library), /WW1/DF/095.

33 Philippa Levine, '"Walking the Streets in a Way No Decent Woman Should": Women Police in World War I', *Journal of Modern History*, vol. 66, no. 1 (1994), p. 45.

34 *Wallasey News*, 3 January 1917.

35 *Bootle Herald*, 19 May 1917.

36 Cecilia Gowdy-Wygant, *Cultivating Victory: The Women's Land Army and the Victory Garden Movement* (Pittsburgh: University of Pittsburgh Press, 2013), p. 40.

37 *Southport Visiter*, 16 July 1918.

3 Problems on the Home Front

1 John Herson, '"Stirring Spectacles of Cosmopolitan animation": Liverpool as a diasporic city, 1825–1913', in Sheryllynne Haggerty, Anthony Webster and Nicolas J. White (eds), *The Empire in One City? Liverpool's Inconvenient Imperial Past* (Manchester: Manchester University Press, 2008), p. 63.

2 *Liverpool Courier*, 18 August 1914.

3 *Liverpool Daily Post*, 20 August 1914.

4 Susan R. Grayzel, *At Home and Under Fire: Air Raids and Culture in Britain from the Great War to the Blitz* (Cambridge: Cambridge University Press, 2012), p. 22.

5 S. S. McClure, *Obstacles to Peace* (Boston: Houghton Miffin, 1917), pp. 157–159.

6 *Quarterly Gazette of the 33rd Liverpool Troop Boys Scouts*, vol. 3, no. 2 (April/June 1916), p. 3.

7 David French, 'Spy Fever in Britain, 1900–1915', *Historical Journal*, vol. 21, no. 2 (1978), 355–370.

8 *Liverpool Courier*, 18 August 1914.

9 *Liverpool Echo*, 14 October 1914.

10 *House of Commons: Parliamentary Debates* (London: HMSO, 1914), 10 August 1916 vol. 85 cc1227-8.
11 Brock Millman, *Pessimism and British War Policy, 1916–1918* (London: Routledge, 2013), p. 79.
12 Labour History Archive (Manchester), WNC 3/4/4/1.
13 Ian Gazeley and Andrew Newell, 'The First World War and Working-Class Food Consumption in Britain', *European Review of Economic History*, vol. 17, no. 1 (2013), p. 73.
14 *Liverpool Daily Post*, 15 February 1918.
15 *Evening Express*, 15 October 1917.
16 Liverpool City Council Minute Book, 67, 1 March 1916, p. 213.
17 Joseph Bibby, *The War its Unseen Cause and Some of its Lessons* (Liverpool: J. Bibby and Sons, 1915), pp. 3, 5–8.
18 K. R. Grieves, 'The Liverpool Dock Battalion: Military Intervention in the Mersey Docks, 1915–1918', *Transactions of the Historical Society of Lancashire and Cheshire*, vol. 131 (1982), p. 148.
19 *Liverpool Daily Post*, 15 March 1915.
20 *Evening Express*, 15 May 1917.
21 *Liverpool Echo*, 6 April 1915.
22 *Manchester Evening News*, 27 June 1917.
23 Fred Bower, *Rolling Stonemason: An Autobiography* (London: Jonathan Cape, 1936), pp. 206, 208–209, 211–12.
24 *Liverpool Daily Post*, 5 April 1918.
25 *The Liverpool, Bottle, Birkenhead and Wallasey Official Red Book 1919* (Liverpool: Littlebury Bros, 1920), p. 593.
26 *Garston and Woolton Weekly News*, 10 May 1918.
27 *Evening Express*, 1 October 1917.
28 Lucy Bland, 'White Women and Men of Colour: Miscegenation Fears in Britain After the Great War', *Gender and History*, vol. 17, no. 1 (2005), p. 50.
29 *Evening Express*, 5 July 1917.
30 *St Helens Newspaper*, 13 November 1917.
31 Watch Committee for the City of Liverpool Report on the Police Establishment and the State of Crime, for the Year Ending 31 December, 1918 (Liverpool: Head Constable's Office, 1919), pp. 10–12, 14.
32 Ernest William Barnes, *Spiritualism and the Christian Faith* (Liverpool: Liverpool diocesan board of divinity publications, 1918), pp. 47–48, 52–53.
33 *Liverpool Daily Post*, 28 August 1917.

34 Edward H. Beardsley, 'Allied Against Sin: American and British Responses to Venereal Disease in World War I', *Medical History*, vol. 20, no. 2 (1976), p. 191.

35 *Public Health*, vol. 31 (1918), pp. 141–2.

36 Adrian Gregory, *The Last Great War: British Society and the Great War* (Cambridge: Cambridge University Press, 2008), p. 235.

37 John Belchem, *Irish, Catholic and Scouse: The History of the Liverpool-Irish, 1800–1939* (Liverpool: Liverpool University Press, 2007), p. 255.

38 *Liverpool Catholic Herald*, 15 May 1915.

4 Entertainment on the Home Front

1 Tony Collins, *Rugby League in Twentieth-Century Britain: A Social and Cultural History* (London: Routledge, 2006), p. 11.

2 *Liverpool Courier*, 5 September 1914.

3 *Ellesmere Port Advertiser*, 26 September 1917.

4 Alethea Melling, '"Ray of the Rovers": The Working-Class Heroine in Popular Football Fiction, 1915–25', *International Journal of the History of Sport*, vol. 15, no. 1 (1998), p. 98.

5 *Liverpool Echo*, 24 January 1918.

6 *Crosby Herald*, 9 March 1918.

7 Matthew Taylor, *The Association Game: A History of British Football* (Harlow: Longman, 2008), p. 122.

8 *Liverpool Echo*, 29 October 1917.

9 *Evening Express*, 1 June 1917.

10 *Liverpool Daily Post*, 12 September 1917.

11 *Crosby Herald*, 15 September 1917.

12 *The Times*, 4 March 1915.

13 *Liverpool Daily Post*, 12 January 1915.

14 *Evening Express*, 15 March 1915.

15 *Birkenhead News*, 17 July 1918.

16 Kimberley A. Reilly, '"A Perilous Venture for Democracy": Soldiers, Sexual Purity, and American Citizenship in the First World War', *Journal of the Gilded Age and Progressive Era*, vol. 13, no. 2 (2014), pp. 223–255.

17 James M. Howard, *History of the 322d Field Artillery* (New York: J. P. Dempsey, 1920), p. 60.

18 *Places of Interest and Amusement for Members of the Naval and Military Forces of the Allies Visiting Liverpool* (Liverpool: Rotary Club, 1918).

19 *Liverpool Daily Post*, 12 December 1914.
20 *Liverpool Daily Post*, 15 April 1916.
21 *St Helens Newspaper*, 7 June 1918.
22 *Crosby Herald*, 8 September 1917.
23 *Liverpool Daily Post*, 25 September 1914.
24 *The Sphinx: A Monthly Magazine for Magicians and Illusionists*, vol. 12 (March, 1913), p. 4.
25 *Liverpool Echo*, 4 February 1916.
26 *Garston and Woolton Weekly News*, 25 June 1915.
27 *Liverpool Daily Post*, 8 August 1916.
28 David Robinson, *Chaplin: The Mirror of Opinion* (Bloomington, Indiana University Press, 1983), p. 17.
29 *Manchester Courier*, 29 September 1914.
30 *Liverpool Daily Post*, 7 May 1918.
31 *Liverpool Echo*, 12 September 1914.
32 *Liverpool Courier*, 22 January 1915.
33 *Deeside Advertiser*, 17 August 1917.
34 *Liverpool Daily Post*, 7 September 1917.
35 *Wallasey News*, 8 August 1914.
36 *Sphinx: Guild of Undergraduates University of Liverpool*, vol. 24, no. 4 (March 1918), pp. 85–86.
37 *Crosby Herald*, 6 July 1918.
38 *Bootle Times*, 29 June 1917.
39 *St Helens Newspaper*, 2 June 1916.

5 Remembering, Celebrating and Commemorating

1 Adrian Gregory, 'Lost generations the impact of military casualties on Paris, London and Berlin', Jay Winter and Jean-Louis Robert (eds), in *Capital Cities at War: Paris, London, Berlin 1914-1919, vol. 1*(Cambridge: Cambridge University Press, 1999), p. 89.
2 *Wallasey News*, 7 July 1917.
3 Alex King, *Memorials of the Great War in Britain: The Symbolism and Politics of Remembrance* (Oxford: Berg, 1998), p. 76.
4 *Dunstan's Parish Magazine: A Monthly Paper for the Congregation and Parishioners of St. Dunstan's, Earle Road, Liverpool* (July 1920), p. 3.
5 *Evening Express*, 7 October 1917.

6 Catherine Moriarty, 'Narrative and the Absent Body: Mechanisms of Meaning in First World War Memorials', PhD thesis, University of Sussex (1995), p. 77.

7 *Birkenhead News*, 9 November 1918.

8 *House of Commons: Parliamentary Debates* (London: Her Majesty's Stationary Office, 1919), 17 December 1919, vol. 123 cc485-512.

9 *Crosby Herald*, 17 March 1917.

10 Labour History Archive (Manchester), WNC 13/4/7/1; WNC 13/4/7/8.

11 *Bootle Times*, 16 November 1918.

12 *Birkenhead News*, 16 November 1918.

13 *Liverpool Echo*, 11 November 1918.

14 Bonnie White, *The Women's Land Army in First World War Britain* (London: Palgrave, 2014), p. 145.

15 *Liverpool Daily Post*, 21 November 1918.

16 Liddle Collection (Leeds University Library) WWI/AIR/ 101.

17 *Liverpool Daily Post*, 21 June 1919.

18 *Liverpool Daily Post*, 28 June 1919.

19 Howard Cochran, 'Hate', in M.E. Buckley (ed.),*The Mail-Bag a Souvenir of the Postal Censor's Office at Liverpool during the Great War* (Liverpool: Daily Post, 1919), p. 53.

20 W. A. Gibson Martin, *A Century of Liverpool's Commerce* (Liverpool: Birchall, 1950), pp. 152–153.

21 Colin G. Pooley and Sandra Irish, 'Access to Housing on Merseyside, 1919–39', *Transactions of the Institute of British Geographers*, vol. 12, no. 2 (1987), p. 180.

22 *Liverpool Daily Post*, 1 September 1919.

23 Sanford Cole, *Our Home Ports* (London: E. Wilson, 1923), pp. 119–121.

24 Rosie Kennedy, *The Children's War: Britain, 1914–1918* (London: Palgrave, 2014), p. 38.

25 Letter in possession of Chris Daly.

26 Imperial War Museum, DS/2423/Eric/Letter 37.

Index